W9-CRO-560

THE BEST OF
Italian Cooking

2/10/99

Spaghetti alla Salsa di Noci
(see recipe p. 37)

THE BEST OF
Italian Cooking

Fiorella de Boos-Smith

BAY BOOKS
Sydney and London

To Catherine Campbell and Kathy Bodnar
who made the English more intelligible while
keeping the Italian flavour.

Photography by Ashley Barber

We gratefully acknowledge the
assistance of: The Bay Tree Kitchen
Shop (Woollahra, NSW) and
Klimbim Kitchenware (Paddington,
NSW).
Tiles from Fred Pazotti (Woollahra,
NSW).

Food prepared and presented by
Voula Kyprianou.

This book is copyright. Apart from
any fair dealing for the purpose of
private study, research, criticism or
review, as permitted under the
Copyright Act, no part may be
reproduced by any process without
written permission. Enquiries
should be addressed to the
publishers.

Published by Bay Books
61–69 Anzac Parade,
Kensington NSW 2033

Publisher: George Barber

Copyright © Bay Books 1984
Revised edition 1985

National Library of Australia
Card Number and ISBN
0 85835 812 3

Gnocchi di Patate
(see recipe p.41)

Contents

Introduction

When one is, like myself, an Italian living in Australia, one listens with great joy and interest to the tales of travellers who have spent a happy holiday in Italy. They speak of her cities and of her villages, of ruins and landscapes, of sea resorts, monuments and art galleries, but I seldom get the impression that these charming tourists have fully experienced and understood the local food.

This is, of course, not as surprising as it sounds, for food in Italy is indeed a difficult subject. The rich variety of dishes, as well as the complexity of customs, of dialects and of traditions have puzzled more than one theorist or scholar set on demonstrating that uniformity is the surest way of testing unity.

Italy became united as a nation in 1854, but in more aspects than one it is still a conglomeration of different, if complementary, regions. In the kitchen department, in particular, we are unable to show the visitor a list of national dishes, but can only produce a collection of regional specialities.

The image of Italians living on pasta, tomatoes and olive oil is, of course, no more true than that of Australians subsisting on meat pies and pavlova. This situation was perhaps started by the proliferation of restaurants outside Italy which call themselves Italian but which in fact create and perpetuate an ethnic tradition of Italian food abroad that is only vaguely connected to the home truth.

The lover of cuisine should inquire, when travelling in Italy, about the local specialities and avoid ordering a steak in Naples, which is on the sea and away from farming areas, or fish in Florence, which is inland and offers marvellous steak.

As for Australia, when reproducing foreign cuisines at home, one must of course compromise and make the best of the local products and substitutes, keeping the integrity of approach.

In this book, I have given a selection of Italian dishes from various regions which have become famous throughout the world. I have also added a few lesser known ones and some that we used to favour in my own household in Trieste, where I grew up. None of them is particularly difficult to prepare, as we traditionally rely on natural flavours rather than complexity of preparation. The estimated time of preparation and cooking, and the degree of difficulty are given for each recipe; + indicates easy, ++ moderately easy, +++ difficult.

All ingredients used in this book are readily available from most supermarkets and delicatessens. I trust you will enjoy the dishes and I wish you "Buon appetito!"

Pollo al Cacciatore
(see recipe p. 80)

7

Ingredients

Herbs
In Italy we use few spices — pepper, nutmeg, saffron, perhaps a few cloves — while herbs, both fresh and dried, play a most important role. The favourite herbs are listed below.
Basil: used to flavour tomato sauce and tomato salad, it is delicious when stewed with green vegetables such as zucchini. The main ingredient of *pesto*, the glorious sauce of Genoa. Used mainly fresh.
Marjoram and Oregano: used, mainly dried, to flavour meat stews and grilled or baked fish. They are the herbs that are sprinkled on pizza toppings.
Mint: used fresh, mainly in Roman cooking, to flavour salads and soup and in the cooking of globe artichokes.
Rosemary: fresh or dried, is the essential aroma for roast meats, particularly lamb, but also pork and chicken. Use sparingly.
Fennel seeds: excellent with cabbage, as a flavouring in salami and other sausages, and added to roast pork.
Parsley: used widely for decoration, stuffing, and mixed with other herbs for soups and stews. Italian parsley is of the flat leaf variety.
Garlic
Italian food is not as heavily garlic-flavoured as one has become accustomed to believe. We prefer to add a couple of garlic cloves to dishes during the cooking rather than at the beginning to avoid the pungent smell it develops in contact with hot butter or oil.

Olive oil
It is used in most dishes in preference to butter, and it can vary from extremely light (*olio di oliva vergine*) to rather heavy, depending on the personal preference of the cook. Olive oil is also used for frying, as it gives a lovely golden colour and appetising smell to food. Italy has been for centuries a great producer of olive oil, which it exports all over the world.
Butter
It is always unsalted and used mainly in the cooking of the north, in the cities near the Po valley, where cattle are raised.
Peeled tomatoes (canned) and tomato paste
Essential to have at hand for a variety of dishes, they are two of the few national concessions to canned food.
Anchovies
They are used in antipasto and to flavour a number of dishes, such as *abbacchio*.
Olives, green and black
They are used widely for snacks and sauces.
Parmesan cheese
If you can afford to splurge, the imported variety is infinitely better.
Wine
Sauces and stews seldom have water added to them. Wine, white or red, and/or tomatoes are usually enough to produce the amount of liquid desired. Wine is also used in the marinating of meats.

HORS D'OEUVRE

Italians are great lovers of antipasto (literally 'before the meal') and travellers to Italy never fail to gasp on entering the best restaurants at the beautiful displays of antipasto colourfully arranged on special tables.

In the following pages you will find a small selection of suitable recipes. But a good antipasto can also be prepared from products bought ready from the delicatessen or the fish market, such as a platter of best quality salami or coppa, some shiny olives, a few hearts of artichokes preserved in oil, fresh oysters presented just with lemon (in Italy oysters are an expensive delicacy and only a maximum of six per person is served), prawns, crab, mussels open and served raw in their shell, mangoes decorating a plate of thinly sliced ham, smoked salmon — the list could go on for ever.

At home, antipasto should be presented in small portions, to stimulate the appetite, and should always be arranged as pleasantly as possible to put the diner in a good mood, and reassure him or her as to the quality of the cooking to follow. As we say in Italian: *Buon appetito!*

Insalata di Calamaretti

Baby Squid Salad

500 g small squid
2 tablespoons white wine vinegar
1 small onion
6 peppercorns
1 lemon
6 tablespoons olive oil
salt and pepper
2 cloves garlic
2 tablespoons chopped parsley
1 green capsicum
4 small gherkins (optional)

Time: 1 hour
Difficulty: +

Clean the squid under running water, discarding the intestines and transparent spine and separating the hood from the tentacles. Rub off the purplish outer skin and rinse under cold water. Cut the hood in thin rings and the tentacles in pieces. Make a bouillon with enough water to cover the squid, the vinegar, quartered onion, salt and peppercorns. Add the squid and boil for 3–5 minutes, depending on size, until just tender. Do not overcook as the squid will toughen. Drain.

In the meantime prepare a dressing with the juice of the lemon, the oil, salt and pepper and crushed garlic. Gently mix the dressing with the still warm squid and add the finely chopped parsley. Decorate with rings of capsicum and chopped gherkins. Serve warm or cold.

Serves 4.

Uova alla Fiorentina

Eggs Florentine Style

8 eggs
300 g cooked spinach or 1 packet frozen spinach
30 g butter
2 tablespoons milk
2 tablespoons grated Parmesan
salt

Time: 30 minutes
Difficulty: +

Preheat the oven to 200°C (400°F).

Melt the butter in a saucepan, add the spinach and sauté until warm through. Mix in the Parmesan cheese, milk and a little salt. Butter 8 individual ramekins and distribute the spinach mixture among them. Now break an egg on top of each ramekin and put in the oven until the whites have become a milky colour and the yolks are just starting to set. Serve immediately with toast fingers.

Serves 8.

Mixed antipasto

Prosciutto Crudo con Melone

Prosciutto Crudo con Melone

Prosciutto and Melon

Prosciutto crudo, or raw ham, can now be found easily in Australia. It should not be too salty, and must always be sliced very thin. A good substitute is *coppa*, which is the shoulder of pork, cured in the same way.

1 honeydew or rock melon

Time: 30 minutes
Difficulty: +

300 g prosciutto, in very thin slices

Arrange the slices of melon on a serving platter and top them with the slices of ham. Serve very cold.
Serves 6.

Acciughe con Peperoni alla Calabrese

Salad of Anchovies and Capsicums in the Calabrian Style

12 anchovy fillets
1 green capsicum
1 yellow capsicum
1 red capsicum
4 hard-boiled eggs
2 tablespoons capers
1 tablespoon chopped parsley
6 tablespoons olive oil

Time: 1 hour
Difficulty: +

With the help of a fork, hold the capsicums, one at a time, over the flame of a gas burner or under a hot grill until the skin is blistered and can easily be rubbed off. Take the seeds out and cut the capsicums in thin strips.

Shell the eggs and chop them finely. Salt lightly.

On a rectangular platter, arrange in neat rows the anchovy fillets and the strips of green, red and yellow capsicums. Fill the spaces between rows with chopped eggs and capers. Sprinkle with parsley and season with olive oil. Serve with hot bread rolls.
Serves 4.

12

Prosciutto con i Fichi

Prosciutto and Figs

As for Prosciutto Crudo con Melone, but substitute fresh peeled figs for the melon.

Pomodori Ripieni di Riso

Tomatoes with Rice

4 large ripe tomatoes
200 g rice
100 g Gruyère cheese
200 g ham
1 small onion

30 g butter
salt and pepper

Time: 1 hour
Difficulty: +

Cook the rice in boiling salted water, being careful to leave it *al dente*, or still a little bit firm. Drain it and mix it with the finely chopped onion, the butter, the ham and the grated cheese, salt and pepper.

Cut a slice off the top of each tomato and scoop out the seeds and flesh.

Fill the tomatoes with the rice mixture, replace the tops and put them in a very hot oven for approximately 15 minutes, until they start to brown. Serve hot.

Serves 4.

Note: Capsicums can be prepared in the same way.

Add onion, butter, ham and cheese to the cooked rice.

Scoop seeds and flesh out of each tomato.

Fill tomatoes with the rice mixture.

Pomodori Ripieni di Riso

Antipasto di Riso, Gamberi e Cozze

Rice Salad with Prawns and Mussels

200 g rice
500 g freshly cooked
    king prawns
1 kg mussels
1 glass dry white wine
2 lemons
6 tablespoons olive oil
pepper
1 small bunch parsley
3 anchovy fillets

Time: 1½ hours (plus time for chilling)
Difficulty: +

Brush the mussels under running water to free the shells of grit. Discard any open ones. Put them in a wide pan with the wine and bring to the boil. Lift them out as soon as they open. Shell approximately half of them, reserving the other half for decoration. Shell the prawns.

Boil the rice in salted water, drain it and run some cold water through it to separate the grains. Season it with the juice of half a lemon, the oil, plenty of pepper, the finely chopped parsley and the chopped anchovy fillets. Add salt if necessary.

Just before serving, stir the prawns into the rice, reserving some for decoration. Arrange the rice in a glass bowl and decorate it with reserved prawns, mussels in shell and lemon slices. Serve very cold.

Serves 4.

Bagna Cauda alla Piemontese

Hot Dip for Raw Vegetables

This is a very popular dip, originally from Piedmont. Serve it hot with a variety of crudités and let guests do their own dipping. Suitable crudités are strips of carrot, celery, fennel, capsicum, shallots, cauliflower florets and zucchini.

5 cloves garlic
2 tablespoons milk
60 g butter
300 mL olive oil
120 g anchovies

Time: 1 hour (apart
    from steeping garlic)
Difficulty: +

Chop garlic very finely and leave it in the milk for a few hours to take away some of its pungency. Put the oil and butter in a heatproof earthenware pot (a fondue pot is suitable), add the finely chopped anchovies and the drained garlic and cook on very low heat for about 15 minutes, stirring from time to time. Serve immediately, with the prepared vegetables.

Serves 4.

Crostini di Fegatini

Crostini with Chicken Livers

8 slices French bread
300 g chicken livers
1 small onion
1 celery stalk
60 g butter
6 tablespoons Marsala
    or sherry
nutmeg
salt and pepper

Time: 30 minutes
Difficulty: +

Chop the onion and celery and sauté in butter until translucent. Add the chicken livers cut in small pieces and sauté for about 3 minutes, so that inside is still pink. Now add the Marsala or sherry, salt, pepper and a generous sprinkle of grated nutmeg. Let it evaporate on high heat until there are only about 2 tablespoons of liquid left.

Fry the bread and top it with the mixture. Serve immediately.

Serves 4.

Ostriche alla Tarantina

Baked Oysters

36 oysters in shell
3 tablespoons finely
chopped parsley
3 tablespoons
breadcrumbs
6 tablespoons olive oil
1½ lemons
freshly ground pepper

Time: 30 minutes
Difficulty: +

Arrange the oysters in a single layer in an oven dish. Sprinkle the parsley on top. Grind a generous quantity of black pepper over them and pour on a little olive oil. Add the breadcrumbs, more freshly ground black pepper and the remainder of the olive oil. Put the oysters in a preheated oven at 160°C (325°F) for 15 minutes. Serve very hot with lemon wedges.
 Serves 6.

Crostini ai Frutti di Mare

Crostini with Hot Seafood

Crostini are a typical feature of Italian snack bars, and the variety of their toppings is endless. At home they are often served between meals or as a light first course.

8 slices French bread
50 g butter
250 g (net weight)
seafood: prawns,
scallops, oysters, etc.
1 clove garlic
1 teaspoon tomato paste
1 tablespoon chopped
parsley or *chopped*
basil
3 tablespoons white
wine
salt and pepper

Time: 1 hour
Difficulty: +

Melt the butter in a small pan and add the finely chopped seafood, the crushed garlic, the tomato paste and the chopped parsley or basil. Moisten with the white wine and simmer for 2 minutes. Add freshly ground pepper and a little salt if necessary.
 Fry the bread in a little oil and top it with the mixture. Serve immediately.
 Serves 4.

Avocado con Gorgonzola

Avocados with Gorgonzola

Gorgonzola is a lovely Italian blue vein cheese, which can be bought from specialist delicatessens in Australia. If unavailable, use your preferred creamy blue vein cheese.

2 large or *4 small*
avocados
100 g Gorgonzola
100 mL vinaigrette,
made out of 3 parts
olive oil to 1 part
vinegar, with salt and
pepper

Time: 30 minutes
Difficulty: +

Cut the avocados in half lengthwise, take out the stone and fill the cavity with the vinaigrette to which the finely chopped cheese has been added.
 Serves 4.

SOUPS AND RICE DISHES

Basically there are two kinds of soup in Italy: those based on a clear meat consommé, to which pasta, rice, small ravioli, dumplings or eggs are added just before eating, and the heavier, more wintry ones, based on vegetables, both fresh and dried. We always eat our soup hot, and serve it instead of pasta, before the main course.

Rice in Italy is eaten mainly in the north, usually in the form of risotto. Good quality Italian rice is now widely available, and I suggest that you buy it when tackling the following recipes. When cooked it develops a most pleasant creaminess, while keeping its *al dente* quality, which is impossible to attain with the local strain.

Risotto in Italy is often served by itself as a first course or else as an accompaniment to a main course.

Minestrone alla Milanese

Vegetable Soup Milanese Style

The variations on this famous soup are endless, depending on the vegetables available and on the imagination of the cook: in fact any or all vegetables in season may be used. If you do not have any meat consommé at hand, a couple of stock cubes would be a suitable substitute.

80 g bacon
80 g butter
1 clove garlic
1 small onion
1 leek
1 sprig rosemary
150 g tomatoes
100 g fresh asparagus
150 g green beans
2 potatoes
2 zucchini
1 celery heart
1.5 L light consommé
salt and pepper
200 g rice
1 small bunch basil or parsley
80 g grated Parmesan

Time: 2 hours
Difficulty: +

Chop the bacon and brown it in the butter together with the chopped garlic, onion and leek. Add the sprig of rosemary and when the mixture starts to look translucent add the peeled and chopped tomatoes. In the meantime clean and chop in small pieces the remaining vegetables and add them to the pan, together with the consommé or water and stock cubes and salt and pepper. Simmer until tender, and then add the rice.

When the rice is cooked but still firm, take the soup off the stove and add the finely chopped basil or parsley and the Parmesan. Let it rest for a few minutes to give time to the flavours to develop, and serve it with some more grated cheese.

Serves 4.

Add chopped tomatoes to the browned garlic, onion and leek.

Add rice when the vegetables are tender.

When cooked, add grated Parmesan.

Pasta e Fagioli

Pasta and Dried Bean Soup

*300 g dried beans
(borlotti), soaked
overnight*
1 small onion
30 g butter
2 tablespoons olive oil
1 carrot
1 stalk celery
parsley
300 g tomatoes
1.5 L water
1 bay leaf

salt and pepper
*200 g pasta (a short
variety is most
suitable)*
80 g Parmesan

*Time: 3½ hours
(excluding time to
soak beans)*
Difficulty: ++

Sauté the chopped onion in the butter and oil until golden, add the finely chopped carrot and celery, the chopped parsley and the peeled and chopped tomatoes. Add the drained beans, the water, bay leaf, salt and pepper. Cook slowly until the beans are tender (about 3 hours).

Now take out about 4 tablespoons of the cooked beans and pass them through a sieve. Put them back into the soup and bring again to the boil. Add the pasta and cook until *al dente*. Before serving, mix through the grated Parmesan.
  Serves 4.

Brodo di Carne

Beef Consommé

*1 kg beef (spare ribs or
shin)*
1 carrot
1 onion
1 stalk celery
1.5 L water
salt
6 peppercorns

Time: 3 hours
Difficulty: +

Put the meat in the cold water, together with all other ingredients, and bring slowly to the boil. Remove the scum that will form on the surface and simmer as gently as possible for 2 hours. You may wish to cool it to remove the fat from the top. Strain it through muslin or a very fine sieve.

This broth should be very clear and all kinds of pasta or rice can be cooked in it before serving. The meat is usually served as the main course (see recipe for Bollito), accompanied with a green sauce and some vegetables.
  Serves 4.

Stracciatella alla Romana

Consommé with Eggs and Semolina

This is a thoroughly delicious soup, very popular all over Italy and very suitable for a formal dinner.

1.5 L beef consommé
2 eggs
*2 tablespoons grated
Parmesan*
*1 tablespoon fine
semolina*
nutmeg

Time: 30 minutes
Difficulty: ++

Beat the eggs in a bowl and add the cheese and semolina to form a smooth batter. Add grated nutmeg.
  Bring the consommé to simmering point and add the mixture slowly, mixing it with a fork while continuing to simmer for about 3 minutes, until soft threads form in the consommé. Eat immediately.
  Serves 4.

Minestra d'Orzo

Barley Soup

150 g pearl barley
80 g smoked bacon
2.5 L water
2 small potatoes
2 large ripe tomatoes
parsley
salt and pepper

Time: 2 hours
Difficulty: ++

Chop the parsley and bacon very finely and place in a pan together with the barley and the water. Simmer slowly for 1 hour. Now add salt and pepper, the potatoes cut in small cubes and the peeled and chopped tomatoes. Continue to simmer for another 30 minutes. Sprinkle with chopped parsley before serving.
Serves 4.

Risotto alla Milanese

Rice Milanese Style

This is the apotheosis of rice dishes and it is essential that it be prepared with Italian arborio rice and best quality saffron.

40 g butter
1 small onion
500 g rice
1 glass dry white wine
1 litre consommé (good
  quality stock cubes
  can be used)
1 good pinch saffron
  strands
100 g grated Parmesan
  cheese
30 g butter extra

Time 1 hour
Difficulty: ++

Sauté the finely sliced onion in 40 g butter until translucent. Add rice, wine and some of the consommé and let the rice absorb it while stirring continuously. Now add the saffron (which you have previously soaked in a little warm water) and the remaining consommé. As soon as the rice is cooked *al dente*, take it off the stove and mix through the remaining butter and the Parmesan. Serve immediately.
Serves 4–6.

Note: The classic Risotto alla Milanese should have the addition of a finely chopped piece of beef marrow (about 30 g for the above quantity). If you can obtain some marrow from your butcher add it to the pan with the onion. Marrow makes the risotto a little creamier.

Risotto alla Milanese

Sauté onions until translucent, then add rice.

Pour in wine and some of the consommé.

Mix in saffron soaked in a little water.

Risi e Bisi

Rice and Pea Soup

This very simple soup is one of the glories of Venetian cooking. It can also be prepared with split peas.

1 onion
2 rashers bacon
1 small bunch parsley
50 g butter
1 kg young peas (about 500 g when shelled)
200 g rice
1.5 L beef or chicken consommé (can be prepared with stock cubes)
200 g grated Parmesan cheese

Time: 2 hours
Difficulty: +

Chop the onion, the bacon and the parsley and sauté in the butter for a few minutes until translucent. Add the shelled peas, cover and cook slowly for about 10 minutes. Now add the rice, and when it has absorbed the butter in the pan, add the consommé. Let it simmer gently until the rice is cooked but still al dente.

Before serving, stir in the Parmesan and some more butter. This soup should be quite thick, with a creamy texture.

Serves 4.

Zuppa di Asparagi

Fresh Asparagus Soup

750 g fresh asparagus
1.5 L water
50 g butter
2 teaspoons flour
2 egg yolks
croûtons

Time: 1 hour
Difficulty: ++

Clean and wash the asparagus spears and cut them into 3 cm pieces. Cook them for 5 minutes in 1.5 L boiling salted water. Drain, reserving the water.

Now make a white roux with the butter and the flour and add the water in which you have cooked the asparagus. Bring to the boil and add the asparagus pieces. Continue to simmer for about 15 minutes.

In a tureen, beat the egg yolks with a tablespoon of water and slowly add the boiling soup, mixing all the time. Serve with croûtons.

Serves 4.

Zuppa Pavese

This very popular soup with historic origins can be a light meal in itself.

It is said that on 24th February 1525, when François I of France lost his battle against the Spaniards near the Pavia's Abbey, he took refuge in a local farmhouse, where he asked for some food. The cook, not wanting to offer such a distinguished visitor the simple farm fare, tried to create something more suitable for a king and voilà — Zuppa Pavese was born.

2 slices bread, fried in butter or toasted and buttered
1 or 2 eggs
1 tablespoon grated Parmesan
1 bowl beef or chicken consommé

Time: 30 minutes
Difficulty: +

Poach the egg in a little consommé, and place it on top of the buttered toast in a bowl. Sprinkle with grated cheese and top up the bowl with more hot consommé. Eat immediately.

Risotto con i Gamberi

Risotto with Prawns

400 g rice
500 g peeled green
*   prawns*
80 g butter
1 tablespoon oil
1 small onion
1 small carrot
1 small celery stalk
1 pinch thyme
1 glass white wine (or a
*   bit more)*
1 small glass brandy

1 litre light consommé
(can be made with
stock cubes)

Time: 1 hour
Difficulty: ++

Melt butter and oil in a heavy pan and sauté finely chopped onion, carrot and celery until translucent. Add thyme and wine and let it simmer until reduced

by half. Add prawns (cut in half if large) and simmer until they change colour — no longer or they will become tough. Take the pan off the stove and flambé with the brandy. Put it aside.

Separately, bring the consommé to the boil and pour in the rice. Cook it until *al dente*. Drain if

necessary and stir through it a tablespoon of butter. Now delicately mix through the prawns and their juice and serve immediately.

Serves 4.

Add prawns to sautéed vegetables.

Pour rice into boiling consommé.

Gently stir prawns into the drained, buttered rice.

Jota

Dried Bean and Sauerkraut Soup

This is a deliciously different soup that originated in Trieste and has now become famous throughout Italy.

200 g dried beans
*   (borlotti)*
1.5 L water or light
*   consommé*
250 g potatoes
1 teaspoon cumin seeds
1 bay leaf
4 tablespoons olive oil
1 level tablespoon flour

2 cloves garlic
250 g sauerkraut

Time: 3 hours
(excluding time to
soak beans)
Difficulty: ++

Soak beans for a few hours or overnight. Drain and cook them in the water together with the peeled and cubed potatoes, adding the cumin and bay leaf.

In a frying pan brown the flour in the oil to which you have added the garlic. Add a small quantity of water to make it into a thick brown roux and add it to the beans and potatoes. When the beans are nearly cooked, add the sauerkraut and simmer for a further twenty minutes. This soup should be quite thick.

Serves 4.

Risotto con i Gamberi

Kitchenware from The Bay Tree Kitchen Shop

Risotto con i Funghi

Risotto with Mushrooms

80 g butter
1 small onion
1 clove garlic
1 sprig rosemary
1 generous pinch
  oregano or *thyme*
300 g button
  mushrooms
1 small glass white wine
400 g rice (arborio)
1 litre consommé (can
  be made with stock
  cubes)
100 mL fresh cream

70 g grated Parmesan
  cheese
freshly ground pepper
salt

Time: 1 hour
Difficulty: ++

Sauté the finely sliced onion, crushed garlic and the herbs in butter until translucent. Add the mushrooms, halved or quartered, depending on size, and the wine, and let it evaporate for a few minutes. Now add the rice and stir it around the pan to let it absorb the flavours. Gradually add the hot consommé and keep stirring, adding more and more as the rice absorbs the liquid. The quantity of consommé depends on the quality of the rice and how you like it cooked. I think it is best when still *al dente* or rather firm. Adjust the seasoning. When you feel that the risotto is cooked enough, take the pan off the stove and add the fresh cream, stirring through delicately. Put the lid on and let it rest for 2 minutes. Serve immediately with grated Parmesan and plenty of freshly ground pepper.
  Serves 4.

PASTA

I am often asked the secret for good pasta. My answer is very simple, though not always popular. I maintain that the first and most important step is to buy imported brands, as the local quality still leaves much to be desired. Good pasta must be made from durum wheat, or it will stick and swell when cooked.

In Italy pasta comes in a hundred different shapes and sizes and each variety has its own name: spaghetti (strings), farfalle (butterflies), conchiglie (shells), penne (nibs), cappelletti (little hats), viti (screws), fettucine (ribbons), and so on. The choice is entirely up to your whim, as they are all made by the same method and should taste the same, although somehow some types seem to go better with a particular sauce than others.

Pasta is not difficult to make at home, and a basic recipe is given below.

∗ Always boil pasta in plenty of salted water (1 litre of water for each 100 g is a good average measure).
∗ Long pasta such as spaghetti or tagliatelle should not be broken. Put the whole sheaf in the water and press it down gently against the bottom of the pan, and it will gradually soften. At this point, curl it round the pan until it is totally submerged in the water.
∗ Do not prepare pasta in advance of your meal.

If you need to keep it warm for a few minutes, place it in a colander over hot water and put a lid or cloth over the colander.
∗ Cooking times vary with different shapes and quality. Pasta must always be cooked *al dente*, that is, it must keep a little bite to it. It should not be mushy. Home-made pasta needs to be boiled only 2–3 minutes; commercial varieties between 5 and 15. The surest test is to lift out a strand and taste it.

Pasta Casalinga

Home-made Pasta

1 kg flour
6 eggs
2 level tablespoons salt
4–5 tablespoons water

Time: 1½ hours
Difficulty: ++

Pour sifted flour into a mound on a bench, make a well in the middle, and break in the eggs. Add salt and start mixing the flour into the eggs, with the help of a knife if you wish. Keep working until you have a doughy ball. If while mixing you feel that the dough is too dry add a little water.

Now start kneading, keeping your hands floured, until the pasta is elastic and does not break off when you pull. Divide the dough into two balls and wrap them in a wet towel. Let it rest in a cool place for about 2 hours.

With a rolling pin, roll out the pastry until it is as thin as a piece of cloth, keeping it always lightly floured. Your pasta is now ready to be cut into any shape desired. For tagliatelle, flour the sheet of dough, roll it up and cut it in thin ribbons. Another popular shape for home-made pasta is *quadrelli* or little squares.

Serves 6.

Break eggs into the sifted flour and mix with a knife.

Work the mixture into a ball and knead until elastic.

Cut thinly rolled pastry into desired shapes.

Pasta Casalinga Verde

Spinach Pasta

To the basic dough add
200 g cooked and very
well strained spinach.

Paglia e Fieno con Burro e Formaggio

Hay and Straw with Butter and Cheese

250 g green tagliatelle
250 g yellow or egg
    tagliatelle
150 g butter at room
    temperature
100 g grated Parmesan
    cheese
salt

freshly ground pepper

Time: 30 minutes
Difficulty: +

Cook together the green
and yellow tagliatelle until
al dente. Drain and place
in a deep serving plate.

Add the butter in little
pieces and half the
Parmesan. Stir through
and serve, passing the
remaining Parmesan
around, together with the
pepper mill.
    Serves 4.

Linguine alla Carbonara

Pasta with Egg and Ham Sauce

This is a delicious and fast
way to serve pasta, and
very suitable for a dinner
party if you can spend a
few minutes in the kitchen
just before serving.

400 g linguine or other
    long pasta
150 g ham
olive oil
4 eggs

120 g grated Parmesan
    cheese
salt and freshly ground
    pepper
6 tablespoons fresh
    cream
40 g butter

Time: 30 minutes
Difficulty: ++

In a small pan brown the
chopped ham in a little
olive oil.
    In the meantime, beat
the whole eggs in a bowl,
together with the cheese,
salt and pepper and the
fresh cream.
    Cook the linguine in
plenty of boiling salted
water and drain. Put it in a

warm serving dish, pour
on the melted butter and
the egg mixture and mix
thoroughly. It is most
important that the serving
dish is warm and the pasta
piping hot so that the eggs
become slightly
scrambled.
    Serves 4.

Penne all'Arrabbiata

Pasta with Chilli

400 g penne (or other
    short pasta)
70 g butter
120 g bacon
200 g button
    mushrooms
2 cloves garlic
1 small chilli
400 g tomatoes, peeled
    and chopped

1 small bunch basil
salt
70 g grated Parmesan
    cheese

Time 1 hour
Difficulty: +

In a heavy pan, sauté the
chopped bacon in the
butter, add the finely
sliced mushrooms and let
them cook for a few
minutes. Now add the
chopped garlic, the chilli,
the tomatoes and the
roughly chopped basil
leaves. Taste for salt and

let the sauce simmer for
15 minutes.
    Cook the pasta in plenty
of boiling salted water.
Drain it and mix with
some extra butter and the
Parmesan cheese. Serve
immediately topped with
the sauce.
    Serves 4.

Cannelloni alla Laziale

Cannelloni with Beef, Bacon and Mushroom Stuffing

For the pastry
400 g flour
4 eggs
1 tablespoon oil
salt

For the filling
40 g butter
1 small onion
1 small carrot
1 celery stalk
250 g minced beef
100 g ham or bacon
100 g fresh mushrooms
1 lamb's or calf's brain
  (optional)
salt, pepper and nutmeg
1 glass dry white wine
1 teaspoon flour
200 g tomatoes, peeled
  and chopped

1 tablespoon chopped
  parsley

For the sauce
50 g butter
1 × 500 g can peeled
  tomatoes
1 teaspoon sugar
salt and pepper
1 clove garlic (optional)

Time: 2½ hours
Difficulty: ++

To make cannelloni, make pastry as described in the recipe for lasagna and cut it into rectangles 10 × 8 cm. Cook the rectangles in boiling salted water for about 2 minutes, being careful not to overcook. Lift them out and place on paper towel to dry.

To make the filling, sauté in butter in a heavy pan the finely chopped vegetables, the beef, the finely chopped bacon, the sliced mushrooms and the chopped brain. Season with salt, pepper and a good pinch of nutmeg. Add wine, flour and tomatoes and cook until the sauce thickens.

To make tomato sauce, warm butter in pan, add puréed tomatoes, sugar, salt, pepper and garlic. Simmer for 5 minutes.

Arrange on each of the pasta squares a heaped tablespoon of filling and roll them up to form cannelloni or tubes. Arrange the cannelloni in a buttered oven dish. If you wish to arrange them in layers, separate each layer with a few spoons of tomato sauce and some grated Parmesan and dot with butter. Pour tomato sauce on top, sprinkle with Parmesan and butter and brown in the oven at 225°C (425°F).
Serves 4.

Cook cannelloni in boiling salted water.

Cook filling until it begins to thicken.

Lasagna

Each family and region have their own preferred recipe for lasagna. The principle remains the same, but the flavour can be varied as you wish. Here are a few suggestions:

* Layer the lasagna with Bolognese sauce and slices of mozzarella cheese. Finish with Parmesan and butter.
* Layer green lasagna with a sauce made with minced beef or veal and 100 g chicken livers. Use the same ingredients and method as for Bolognese sauce, omitting the tomatoes.
* Layer green or yellow lasagna with a mixture of seafood lightly cooked in butter added to a thick béchamel sauce. Sprinkle each layer with parsley and Parmesan or Gruyère.

Lasagna Pasticciata con Prosciutto e Funghi
Lasagna with Ham and Mushrooms

For the pastry
400 g flour
4 eggs
1 tablespoon oil
salt

For the sauce
100 g butter
1 small onion
1 carrot
1 celery stalk
250 g lean minced veal
   or beef
300 g fresh mushrooms
200 g tomatoes, peeled
   and chopped
salt and pepper
100 g ham
100 g grated Parmesan
   cheese
1 small bunch parsley

Time: 2½ hours
Difficulty: +++

Sift flour and form into a mound on a bench, make a well in the middle and break in the eggs. Add salt and oil and mix and knead until you have an elastic ball. Wrap it in a slightly wet towel and let it rest for 30 minutes. With a rolling pin, roll out the pastry until it is as thin as a piece of cloth, keeping it lightly floured all the time. Now cut it into 8 cm squares and arrange them flat on a floured surface to dry.

Chop the onion, carrot and celery finely and sauté in 15 g butter. Add the minced meat, the finely sliced mushrooms, the chopped parsley and the tomatoes. Add salt and pepper and a little water or white wine and let it cook for 25 minutes.

Cook the lasagna, a few at a time, in plenty of boiling salted water, being most careful not to overcook (it will take only about 2 minutes). Lift out and arrange on a kitchen towel to dry.

Butter an ovenproof dish and arrange in layers the lasagna, some sauce, strips of ham and some Parmesan, and dot each layer with butter. Finish with Parmesan and butter. Put the dish in the oven at 225°C (425°F) until it is brown on top.

Serves 4.

Cut thinly rolled pastry in squares or rectangles.

Sauté vegetables, then add meat, tomatoes and mushrooms.

Arrange layers of lasagna, sauce, ham and Parmesan in an ovenproof dish.

Spaghetti alla Puttanesca
Spaghetti with Anchovies and Capers

400 g spaghetti
40 g butter
olive oil
2 cloves garlic
4 anchovy fillets
150 g black olives
1 tablespoon capers
4 tomatoes
salt and pepper
1 tablespoon chopped
    parsley

Time: 1 hour
Difficulty: +

In a heavy pan, warm the butter with a little oil and sauté the garlic cloves cut in thin slices, the chopped anchovies, the stoned and chopped olives, the chopped capers, the peeled and chopped tomatoes. Cook slowly for 15 minutes.

Boil the spaghetti in plenty of water, drain and arrange on a serving plate. Pour the sauce on top and sprinkle with chopped parsley. Serve immediately.

Serves 4.

Fettuccine Alfredo

This fettuccine dish was made famous by Alfredo at his Roman restaurant, a favourite eating and meeting place of film stars.

400 g fettuccine
120 g butter
200 g ham, diced
200 g sliced button
    mushrooms
3 tablespoons finely
    chopped parsley
300 mL thickened
    cream
100 g grated Parmesan
    cheese
salt and freshly ground
    pepper
extra Parmesan for
    serving

Time: 30 minutes
Difficulty: +

Melt the butter in a heavy frying pan and add diced ham, mushrooms and parsley. Stir over low heat for 1 minute, then add cream. Add Parmesan cheese, salt and lots of freshly ground pepper.

Cook the fettuccine in plenty of boiling salted water. Drain and add to the sauce in the frying pan. Cook gently together for a minute or so, stirring the fettuccine to coat it with the sauce. Serve immediately with more Parmesan.

Serves 4.

Ravioli and Tortellini

These are very tricky to make at home. It is possible to buy good quality ravioli and tortellini from the frozen food section of better supermarkets and continental delicatessens.

Trenette al Pesto

Fettuccine with Pesto Sauce

Pesto is a traditional sauce of Genoa and, apart from its delicious flavour, it is most exquisitely perfumed.

400 g fettuccine
30 g grated pecorino cheese (from continental delicatessens, sometimes sold as Romano)

For the sauce
1 bunch fresh basil
40 g pecorino cheese
40 g grated Parmesan cheese
3 cloves garlic
olive oil
1 tablespoon pine nuts
salt

Time: 1 hour
Difficulty: ++

In a food processor, put the basil leaves, a pinch of salt, the garlic and the cheeses. Whizz while adding enough olive oil to make a rather thick paste. Now add the pine nuts and whizz for another few seconds.

Cook the fettuccine in plenty of boiling salted water until *al dente*. Drain, reserving a couple of tablespoons of the water. In a serving plate, mix the pasta with the reserved water and the pecorino. Now add the pesto and mix again thoroughly. Serve immediately.

Serves 4.

Spaghetti alla Salsa di Noci

Spaghetti with Walnut Sauce

400 g spaghetti
80 g butter
80 g grated Parmesan cheese

For the sauce
100 g walnuts
50 g pine nuts
80 g butter (or olive oil if preferred)
60 g Parmesan cheese
30 basil leaves, chopped finely
2 cloves garlic
salt and pepper

Time: 1 hour
Difficulty: +

Using a pestle or a food processor, reduce the walnuts and pine nuts to a very fine pulp. In a saucepan, heat the butter until it foams and turns brown. Add the nuts and stir for a few seconds. Remove from heat and add grated cheese, salt, pepper and basil. Now gradually add a small quantity of hot water and olive oil until you have obtained a sauce of medium consistency.

Boil the spaghetti in plenty of salted water, drain it and mix it with the butter and Parmesan cheese. Add the sauce and stir gently to coat the strands. Serve immediately.

Serves 4.

Spaghetti alla Bolognese

Spaghetti with Bolognese Sauce

There are many recipes for Bolognese sauce, but the one that follows is the classic one.

400 g spaghetti
100 g grated Parmesan
*   cheese*
70 g butter

For the sauce
400 g best quality mince
4 tablespoons olive oil
100 g bacon
1 onion
1 carrot
1 stalk celery
1 clove garlic

20 g dried mushrooms
*   (obtainable at most*
*   continental*
*   delicatessens)*
1 glass red wine
chopped parsley
chopped marjoram
½ teaspoon grated
*   nutmeg*
salt and pepper
2 tablespoons
*   concentrated tomato*
*   purée*

Time: 1½ hours
Difficulty: +

Soak the mushrooms in a little tepid water for 30 minutes. Drain and chop into small pieces. Heat oil in a pan and add the finely chopped bacon, the chopped onion, carrot, celery and garlic. Sauté until it starts to brown. Add the meat and stir gently for a few minutes. Add the mushrooms and the wine and let the mixture evaporate for a few minutes. Now add the parsley, marjoram, nutmeg, salt, pepper and tomato purée. Stir carefully and add enough water to make a fairly thick sauce. Simmer for 30 minutes.

Cook the spaghetti in plenty of salted water until *al dente*. Drain and transfer it to a deep serving plate. Season it with the butter, half the Parmesan and half the sauce. Pass the rest of the Parmesan and the rest of the sauce round at the table.

Serves 4.

Malfatti alla Fiorentina

Spinach and Cheese Dumplings

These delicious cheese dumplings are easy to make and are always welcomed with admiration by guests. They make an ideal first course for a more formal dinner.

1 kg spinach
300 g ricotta cheese
3 tablespoons grated
*   Parmesan cheese*
3 eggs
salt, pepper and nutmeg

3 tablespoons flour
100 g butter

Time: 1 hour
Difficulty: +++

Cook spinach in a small quantity of water, drain and squeeze thoroughly. Chop finely and add the ricotta and Parmesan cheeses, the whole eggs, salt, pepper and nutmeg.

With your fingers form small dumplings (about the size and shape of a wine cork) and flour them carefully as they will be rather soft. If you have time to let the mixture chill in the refrigerator, you will find the dumplings easier to shape. When they are ready, drop them a few at a time in boiling salted water for about two minutes. They are cooked when they rise to the surface and have hardened. Drain the malfatti and arrange them on a buttered serving dish. Pour some melted butter on top, sprinkle with Parmesan and serve immediately.

Serves 4.

Mix together cheese, eggs, spinach and seasoning.

Form into cork-shaped dumplings.

Cook a few at a time in boiling salted water.

Gnocchi di Semolino alla Romana

Semolina Dumplings

1 litre milk
250 g semolina
120 g butter
salt and pepper
nutmeg
120 g Parmesan cheese
3 egg yolks

Time: 2 hours
Difficulty: ++

Bring the milk to the boil and steadily add the semolina. Add butter, salt, pepper and nutmeg and keep stirring until you have a thick mixture resembling porridge. This will take about 12–15 minutes. The quantity of milk depends on the quality of the semolina. Remove from the heat and add the Parmesan and the egg yolks, stirring with a wooden spoon. Grease a large metal tray or dish and pour the mixture onto it. Spread to a thickness of 1 cm and allow to cool.

Cut the mixture into rounds 4 cm in diameter and arrange, slightly overlapping, in a well buttered ovenproof dish.

Sprinkle generously with Parmesan and melted butter and bake in the oven at 180°C (350°F) until a lovely slightly golden crust forms. Serve alone or as an accompaniment to roast duck or roast chicken.

Serves 4.

Add semolina to the boiling milk.

Spread semolina mixture on a greased tray.

Cut mixture into rounds and arrange in an ovenproof dish.

Gnocchi di Patate

Potato Dumplings

1 kg old potatoes (red
  skins)
30 g butter
2 eggs
300 g plain flour
salt and pepper

Time: 2 hours
Difficulty: +++

When preparing this dish it is important to work quickly so that you are always handling warm dough.

Boil the potatoes in their skins. Drain, and then peel and purée them. Whilst the potatoes are hot, mix in the butter, eggs and flour until a dry yet firm dough is formed. Season with salt and pepper and knead.

Take a ball of dough and roll it with your hands until it is the thickness of a finger and about a metre long. Cut into 2–3 centimetre pieces.

Place one piece in the palm of your hand and gently make a dimple in the dough with your thumb. Using a fork, prick the dough in a pattern and place on a floured towel. Repeat until all dough is used.

Divide the pieces of dough into 2 even lots.

Boil some lightly salted water in a large pan and drop the gnocchi in one by one. As each gnocchi rises to the surface, remove using a slotted spoon. This usually takes about 2–3 minutes. Keep the dumplings warm while the cooking procedure is repeated.

Roll dough until it is about the thickness of a finger.

Cut into pieces and make a dimple in each.

Remove cooked gnocchi from boiling water with a slotted spoon.

PIZZA

In the last few decades the pizza has become part of our popular culture, a fast food that can be a horrible experience or a memorable treat, depending on the chef's invention, or lack of it.

Pizza probably originated in Naples where, to this day, the bakers at the end of many hours of baking relax and prepare themselves a snack. It consists of a piece of bread dough flavoured with whatever additions are available, most commonly some tangy tomatoes, some cheese, a few anchovies, and there it is: the original and true pizza.

All toppings are available nowadays in Pizzaland, from mushrooms and prawns to fried eggs and bacon, but the so-called *Pizza Napoletana* or Neapolitan Pizza is still surely one of the best, and the basis for all the others. The time and difficulty rating given to Pizza Napoletana applies to all the pizza recipes.

Pizza Napoletana

Neapolitan Pizza

For the dough
500 g flour
30 g fresh yeast
salt
2 tablespoons oil

For the topping
500 g tomatoes, fresh or
  canned, peeled and
  coarsely chopped
2 small mozzarellas or
  1 large one
1 can anchovies
oregano
olive oil

Time: 2 hours (plus the time necessary for the dough to rise)
Difficulty: ++

To prepare the dough, sift the flour on to a bench, make a small well in the centre and crumble in the yeast. Mix with a little warm and slightly salted water and the oil until you have a rather soft dough. Knead the dough until it is smooth and elastic and does not stick to the working surface. Form a ball and with a knife cut a cross on its top, to facilitate the rising process. Cover with a clean towel and put in a warm place until it has risen to twice its volume (probably 3 hours).

Flour your working surface and knead the dough again for several minutes. Divide the dough into four and roll each piece out to a thickness of 1 cm or less to form four pizzas. Slightly oil a flat oven tray and place the pizzas on it. Now proceed with the topping.

Cover the pizzas with the chopped tomatoes and then arrange thick slices of mozzarella on top. Decorate with anchovies in a criss-cross pattern, sprinkle generously with oregano and olive oil and cook in the oven at 225°C (425°F) for 30–40 minutes. Eat hot.

Serves 4.

Cut a cross in the dough and leave to rise.

Divide dough into four and roll to 1 cm thick.

Decorate with anchovies.

Pizza con i Funghi

Pizza with Mushrooms

For the dough
the same as Pizza
   Napoletana

For the topping
500 g tomatoes, fresh or
   canned
500 g button
   mushrooms
100 g grated Parmesan

olive oil
salt and pepper

Make the pizza as explained in the recipe for Pizza Napoletana. Cover with the chopped tomatoes and the clean and finely sliced mushrooms. Sprinkle the grated Parmesan on top and season with salt and lots of freshly ground pepper. Sprinkle with a generous amount of olive oil and put it in the oven at 225°C (425°F) for 30–40 minutes.

Serves 4.

Pizza Quattro Stagioni

Four Seasons Pizza

For the dough
the same as Pizza
   Napoletana

For the topping
2 tablespoons tomato
   paste
1 teaspoon dried
   oregano
300 g button
   mushrooms
150 g ham
⅛ teaspoon oregano
1 onion
500 g chopped tomatoes

1 large mozzarella
10 peeled green king
   prawns
1 tablespoon chopped
   parsley
2 tablespoons olive oil

Make the dough as for Pizza Napoletana and line a medium sized pizza tray. Spread tomato paste over dough and sprinkle with oregano.

With a sharp knife, make a slight incision on the pizza and divide into 8 sections.

On the first section arrange some of the sliced mushrooms. On the second, the diced ham, oregano and chopped onion. On the third, chopped tomatoes and grated mozzarella, and on the fourth, chopped tomatoes, sliced green prawns and chopped parsley. Repeat for the remaining four sections of the pizza.

Sprinkle with olive oil and bake in a moderately hot oven (225°C, 425°F) for 30–40 minutes.

Serves 4.

Pizza Margherita

Margherita was the first Queen of Italy and this pizza reflects the colours of the Italian flag: white, red and green.

For the dough
the same as Pizza
   Napoletana

For the topping
500 g tomatoes (or
   canned peeled
   tomatoes)
2 large mozzarellas
300 g green olives
oregano
olive oil

Make the dough as in the preceding recipe. Cover the pizzas with the tomatoes, then thick slices of mozzarella and finally the stoned green olives. Sprinkle with oregano and olive oil and bake as above.

Serves 4.

Pizza con Prosciutto e Olive

Pizza with Ham and Olives

For the dough
the same as Pizza
   Napoletana

For the topping
200 g ham
200 g Gruyère

120 g black olives
olive oil
salt and pepper

Make the dough as explained in the recipe for Pizza Napoletana. Cover with thin strips of ham and the coarsely grated cheese. Dot with the olives and season with a little salt and plenty of freshly ground pepper. Sprinkle generously with olive oil and bake as above.

Serves 4.

FISH AND SEAFOOD

A great quantity of fish of every shape and kind is consumed daily in Italy. Italy is situated right in the middle of the Mediterranean and the greatest number of her cities are either on the seashore or have easy access to it. The catch of the day is bought mainly from the fish markets and it is impossible not to be attracted by the colours and smells, the festive atmosphere and the noises of vendors and buyers alike.

Because fish is always so fresh, Italians tend to cook it very simply and not to bury its sea flavour in sauces and lengthy preparations. It is mainly served with a green salad, never with chips and rarely with cooked vegetables. I have kept the number of recipes in this chapter small, and I have preceded my choice with advice on how to grill and fry fish. Also, as most varieties of fish available in Australia are different from those of Italy, I have suggested suitable local ones.

Cozze alla Marinara

Mussels Marinara

1 kg mussels
2 tablespoons chopped parsley
200 mL dry white wine
120 mL olive oil
salt
cracked pepper
2 tablespoons tomato paste
juice of 1 lemon

Time: 1 hour
Difficulty: +

Clean and wash mussels, discarding any that are open. Put them in a heavy pan with the parsley, wine, salt and pepper. As soon as they open, lift them out. Add tomato paste to the liquid and reduce it to half its quantity.

Replace mussels in pan, add the oil and lemon and heat for 2 minutes so that the mussels absorb the flavour of the liquid.

Serve mussels immediately with their liquid.

Serves 4.

Aragoste Maria Jose di Savoia

Lobster Maria Jose of Savoy

This was one of the favourite dishes of the last Queen of Italy, and she often served it at official banquets.

2 green lobsters or crayfish of about 750 g each
150 g butter
1 small onion
1 small carrot
1 celery stalk
salt and pepper
2 eggs
80 mL fresh cream
1 sprig fresh tarragon

Time: 2 hours
Difficulty: +++

Split the lobsters in half lengthwise and devein them, keeping the coral and creamy parts.

In a small pan, melt 20 g of the butter and to it add the chopped onion, carrot and celery, a little salt and pepper and allow to brown slightly. Off the stove, add 100 g butter and the reserved coral and creamy parts, mixing thoroughly until you have a creamy sauce.

Beat the egg yolks with the fresh cream in a bowl, place the bowl over a pan of simmering water, and gradually add the sauce, mixing all the time. Be very careful that it does not curdle. As soon as it has thickened enough to coat the back of a spoon, remove from the heat and let it rest.

With the remaining butter, brush the lobster halves and put them under the grill, about 20 cm away from the source of heat. Cook evenly for about 20 minutes, brushing them from time to time with more butter.

When they are cooked, pour the egg sauce on top, decorate with sprigs of tarragon and place in the oven at 225°C (425°F) to allow a golden crust to form on top. Serve hot, with a fresh salad seasoned with oil, lemon and salt.

Serves 4.

Pesce al Cartoccio

Fish in a Paper Case

This is an ideal way to cook the more delicate fish as it preserves all the flavour. Serve the fish in its paper case and do the unwrapping at the table.

1 snapper or reef fish, weighing about 1.2 kg
25 g dried mushrooms (available from continental delicatessens) or 150 g button mushrooms
25 g butter
1 clove garlic
2 tablespoons finely chopped parsley
50 g prosciutto or bacon
salt and pepper
oil

Time: 2 hours
Difficulty: ++

Soak the mushrooms in a little warm water, drain, chop and sauté in the butter, together with the crushed garlic clove. Add a couple of tablespoons of the water in which you have soaked the mushrooms and cook slowly for a few minutes. Now add the parsley and prosciutto or bacon in thin strips, take it off the heat and let it rest.

Clean the fish, season it with salt, pepper and oil and arrange it on a sheet of greaseproof paper. Put the mushroom and prosciutto mixture on top and seal the paper so that it forms a bag from which no juices can escape. Place the fish in the oven at 180°C (350°F) and let it cook for about 30 minutes. Serve it with sauté button mushrooms and a fresh salad. You might also need some bread to soak up the delicious juices which will have formed.

Serves 4.

Add prosciutto or bacon to sautéed mushrooms.

Arrange mixture on top of the cleaned fish.

Fold paper to make a sealed bag.

Brodetto alla Triestina

Fish Stew as cooked in Trieste

Each region in Italy has its own version of fish stew or bouillabaisse, often made with the less expensive varieties of fish. It should always include two or more kinds of squid and some crustaceans, as well as a selection of fish of the day.

1 kg mixed fish (prawns, calamari, cuttlefish, mussels, whiting, redfish, leatherjacket, etc.)
2 tablespoons tomato paste
2 cloves garlic
2 tablespoons chopped parsley
2 tablespoons white wine vinegar
100 mL olive oil
1 small glass white wine
salt and pepper

Time: 2 hours
Difficulty: ++

Clean and scale fish and cut in pieces if too big. Shell seafood. Slice calamari and cuttlefish into rings.

Warm the oil in a heavy saucepan. If using cuttlefish, put it in the pan first, as it takes longer to cook, and sauté for about 10 minutes depending on size. Then add all fish and calamari, keeping prawns and mussels for later. Add the wine and continue to cook on a slow heat. When it looks nearly cooked, add the shellfish and simmer for a further 2 minutes. With a slotted spoon, lift out all fish and shellfish and put in a bowl or plate.

To the remaining juices in the pan add the sliced onion, the garlic and the parsley and let them sweat for a few minutes. Now add the tomato paste and 200 mL warm water and simmer for 40 minutes. Then add the fish and the vinegar, test for salt and pepper and continue cooking for another 10 minutes. Serve immediately.

Serves 4.

Note: This dish can also be prepared in advance and reheated.

Calamaretti Ripieni al Forno

Stuffed Baked Squid

This dish is a bit troublesome to prepare but delicious. Try it at least once, and your family will ask you for a repeat performance!

800 g calamari (a 15 cm hood is ideal)
1 clove garlic
1 small bunch parsley

2 or 3 tablespoons fresh breadcrumbs
½ glass dry white wine
oil
salt and pepper
1 egg yolk

Time: 2 hours
Difficulty: ++

Clean the calamari, but leave head intact. Chop the tentacles finely, together with the garlic and the parsley. Add the breadcrumbs, a tablespoon of olive oil, salt and pepper and the yolk of egg. Stuff the heads with this mixture and close them with a toothpick. Arrange the stuffed calamari in an oven dish, moisten with melted butter or oil and sprinkle a little white wine and some salt and pepper on top. Bake at 180°C (350°F) for 40–50 minutes. Serve hot.
   Serves 4.

Finely chop tentacles, garlic and parsley.

Combine ingredients for stuffing.

Stuff heads and close with a toothpick.

Calamaretti Fritti

Fried Small Squid

800 g small calamari
2 lemons
a little flour
oil
salt

Time: 1 hour

Difficulty: +

To clean calamari, separate the tentacles from the head. Empty and clean the head under running water and slice into rings. Throw away the hard beak at the bottom of the tentacles and separate them. Dry the clean calamari pieces and flour them lightly. Heat enough oil to just cover them and when it starts to smoke, throw in the calamari and fry until just golden. Serve immediately, with parsley and lemon.
   Serves 4.

Pesce in Saor

Cold Marinated Fish

800 g small fish fillets (redfish, whiting)
100 mL olive oil
flour
2 tablespoons white wine vinegar
500 g white onions
1 sprig rosemary
1 bay leaf
grated peel of 1 lemon

salt and pepper

Time: 1½ hours (plus time for refrigeration)
Difficulty: +

Shallow fry the floured fillets in half the oil. Drain and arrange in a dish. Add the rest of the oil to the pan together with the thinly sliced onion and sweat slowly, together with the rosemary and crumbled bay leaf. When the onion is cooked, but not brown, add the vinegar and 2 tablespoons of water and let it evaporate to half its quantity. Mix through the lemon peel. Pour this marinade on the cooked fillets and refrigerate for a day before serving. Serve with hot crusty bread to soak up the juices.
   Serves 4.

50

Acciughe Fresche al Finocchio

Fresh Anchovies with Fennel Seeds

*800 g fresh anchovies or
  sardines
100 mL olive oil
2 cloves garlic
1 teaspoon fennel seeds
salt*

*Time: 1 hour
Difficulty: +*

To clean the anchovies or sardines, pull their heads off together with the intestines. Scrape off any scales with your fingers and wash the fish briefly. Dry very carefully with paper towel.

In a wide pan or a frying pan with lid, put the oil and the garlic on low heat, not allowing the garlic to brown. As soon as the oil is warm put in the anchovies and the fennel seeds. Season with a little salt. Cook very, very slowly for 15 minutes, checking from time to time that they are not sticking to the bottom of the pan. Serve with toasted slices of crusty bread.

Serves 4.

Acciughe in Cotoletta

Fresh Anchovy Cutlets

*800 g fresh anchovies or
  sardines
150 g butter
2 eggs
breadcrumbs
salt*

*Time: 1 hour
Difficulty: +*

Clean the anchovies as above and open them to remove the backbone. Wash them briefly and dry carefully. Beat the eggs with the salt, and coat the anchovies first with egg mixture and then breadcrumbs. Fry them slowly in the butter until golden. Serve with anchovy sauce.

Serves 4.

Clean anchovies and remove the backbone.

Coat anchovies first with egg and then breadcrumbs.

Fry in butter until golden.

Salsa di Acciughe

Anchovy Sauce

*3 hard-boiled eggs
4 anchovy fillets
oil
white wine vinegar*

*Time: 30 minutes
Difficulty: +*

Pass the hard-boiled yolks through a sieve together with the anchovy fillets. Add oil and vinegar to taste. Use the finely chopped whites for decoration.

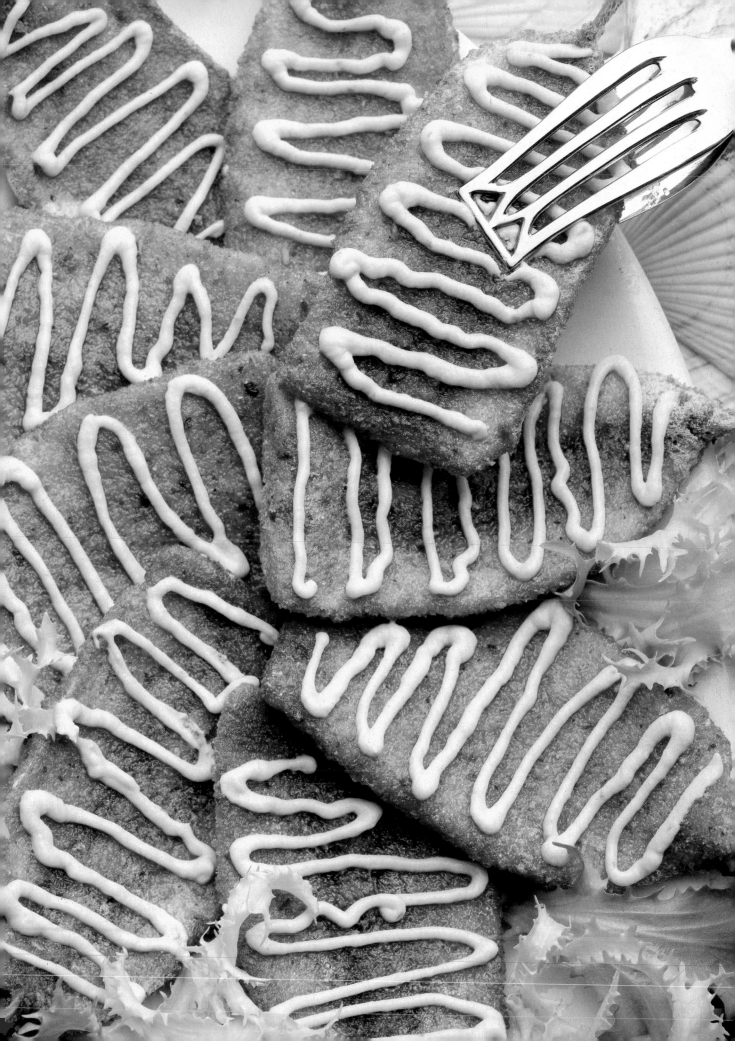

Pesce alla Griglia

Grilled Fish

Suitable for a large fish, grilling is also a good way to prepare the more oily-fleshed varieties such as mullet. If you do not wish to use a barbecue or griller, fish prepared in this way is also delicious baked in the oven.

After cleaning and scaling the fish, wash it briefly and dry it carefully with paper towel. Now place it on a plate and sprinkle with lemon juice, salt, pepper and olive oil, both outside and inside. Leave to marinate for about 15 minutes or so, turning from time to time. Put the fish under a preheated grill. Start the cooking on very high heat so that the skin becomes crisp, and then lower the heat and proceed slowly until the eye turns opaque. If the fish starts to look too dry, brush with some of the marinade. Turn the fish and proceed to cook the other side in the same way. The fish is cooked when the flesh is white throughout and detaches easily from the bones.

When cooked, arrange on a serving plate and sprinkle with lots of chopped parsley to which you have added a clove or two of finely chopped or crushed garlic, a little more salt and pepper and a generous quantity of olive oil. Serve it decorated with lemon slices and a sprig of parsley in its mouth.

Filetti di Pesce con Melanzane

Fish Fillets with Eggplant

8 fish fillets (bream, dory, whiting, etc.)
oil
1 lemon
salt and pepper
1 large eggplant
flour
1 egg
50 g butter

For the garlic butter
100 g butter
50 g garlic

Time: 2 hours
Difficulty: ++

To make the garlic butter, peel the garlic cloves and boil them for 30 seconds in a little water. Cream the butter and incorporate the crushed garlic cloves.

Marinate the fish fillets for 30 minutes or more in a little oil, lemon, salt and pepper, turning from time to time.

Cut the eggplant lengthwise in 8 slices 1 cm thick. Coat with flour and beaten egg and fry them in butter until golden. Grill the fish fillets, and rest each one on a slice of eggplant. Decorate each fillet with garlic butter.
Serves 4.

Pesce con le Olive

Fish with Olives

This is an ideal way to cook a whole snapper or other fine fish.
1 snapper about 1.2 kg
flour
100 mL olive oil
2 cloves garlic
1 tablespoon white wine vinegar
salt and pepper
200 g black olives
Time: 1½ hours
Difficulty: +
Clean the fish, scale it, wash it briefly and dry it carefully. Season lightly and coat with flour. Shake off the excess. In a wide pan, heat the olive oil, and when it starts to smoke, put in the fish and fry it at high heat for a couple of minutes on each side to seal the skin. Now lower the heat, add the crushed garlic, the vinegar and seasoning and cover it with a lid. When the fish looks nearly cooked (the eye will look like a white pearl) add the stoned olives and shake the pan, so that the flavour of the olives penetrates the fish.

To serve, arrange the snapper on a heated serving dish, decorate with the olives, and pour the cooking juices over it.
Serves 4.

Pesce Fritto

Fried Fish

Frying is most suitable for small fish and fillets. After cleaning and scaling the fish, wash it briefly and dry it carefully with paper towel. Warm enough olive or other oil to just cover the fish and when it starts to smoke, put in the lightly floured fish. For small fish and prawns cook at very high heat. For larger fish, lower the heat slightly to allow to cook through, but increase it again towards the end so that the skin becomes crisp. (In Italy we like to eat the skin too.) If you have a large fish and wish to serve it fried, cut it in thick pieces or slices, fry as above, and put it together again on the serving plate.

Fish is cooked when the flesh has become white throughout and detaches easily from the bones. Drain the fish on paper towel, arrange on a heated platter, salt it slightly and serve immediately decorated with fresh parsley and lemon wedges.

Filetti di Sogliola con Zucchine

Fillets of Sole with Zucchini

8 fillets of sole (whiting,
*   dory or barramundi)*
350 g zucchini
oil
1 sprig rosemary
12 leaves fresh basil
salt and pepper
150 g tomatoes, peeled
*   and chopped*
a little flour
80 g butter
breadcrumbs
1 lemon

Time: 2 hours
Difficulty: +

Slice the zucchini and
sauté in a little oil with the
rosemary, basil, salt and
pepper. When nearly
done, add the tomatoes
and sauté for a further 2
minutes.

Flour the fillets of sole
and brown in butter.
Butter an ovenproof dish
and arrange the fillets in
one row if possible. Cover
with the zucchini, sprinkle
with breadcrumbs, dot
with butter and put in the
oven at 225°C (425°F) for
a few minutes until brown.
Serve decorated with basil
leaves and lemon.

Serves 4.

Pesce Freddo con Olio e Limone

Cold Fish with Oil and Lemon

1 snapper or other
*   whole fish, about*
*   1.2 kg*
1 carrot
1 onion
1 celery stalk
1 bay leaf
6 peppercorns
100 mL olive oil
3 lemons
salt and pepper
3 tablespoons chopped
*   parsley*

Time 1 hour (plus time
*   for cooling)*
Difficulty: +

Clean and scale the fish.
Make a court bouillon by
simmering for 30 minutes
the carrot, onion, celery,
bay leaf and peppercorns
in slightly salted water
(enough to cover the fish).
Simmer the fish in the
court bouillon until just
cooked and allow to cool
in its own liquid.

In the meantime
prepare a sauce with the
oil, lots of lemon juice,
salt, pepper and chopped
parsley.

Drain the fish and
arrange on a serving
platter. Decorate it with
sprigs of parsley and pour
half the sauce on top.
Serve the rest of the sauce
separately. If you prefer,
fish prepared this way is
also good with a home-
made mayonnaise.

Serves 4.

Filetti di Sogliola con Zucchine

VEGETABLES

The concept of *piatto con contorno* or 'plate with accompaniment', is relatively recent, dating perhaps from two or three hundred years ago. In the olden days of Greece and the Roman Empire, the common people would eat mainly vegetables. But at the tables of the rich, sometimes a particular vegetable would accompany a meat dish. We know in fact that eel was eaten in Greece with beetroot, and that stewed fig leaves were served with meat. In the *Satyricon* by Petronius Arbiter (first century A.D.) we can read of asparagus with roast birds and of silver beet with sucking pig.

Italians have always been avid consumers of vegetables. Apart from serving them as an accompaniment to meat and fish dishes, they often eat vegetables as a separate course, either at the beginning of the meal or as a main course. Most of the following recipes are in fact suitable to be served also as the beginning of a meal, or as part of a mixed antipasto.

Peperonata

Capsicum Casserole

800 g large capsicum, a mixture of green, yellow and red
100 mL olive oil
200 g sliced onions
2 cloves garlic
2 bay leaves
salt and pepper
500 g peel and chopped tomatoes

Time: 1 hour
Difficulty: +

Wash the capsicum, open them and throw away the seeds. Cut them in large slices.

In a heavy frying pan with a lid, warm the oil and sauté the onions, and the finely sliced garlic and the crushed bay leaves. When the onion is starting to colour, add the capsicums, salt and pepper and continue to sauté for another 10 minutes on fairly high heat. Now add the tomatoes and check the seasoning. Cover the pan with a lid and continue cooking until the capsicum is soft and the tomatoes have formed a thickish sauce. Serve hot or cold.

Serves 4.

Carciofi alla Giudea

Globe Artichokes Jewish Style

This is a very easy dish to cook and is delicious when young tender globe artichokes are available. Although its name indicates its ancient Jewish origins, it is considered one of the glories of Roman cooking and is available at most restaurants of that city in late summer and early autumn.

8 small globe artichokes
oil for deep frying
salt and pepper

Time: 1 hour
Difficulty: ++

Discard the outside woody leaves of the artichokes, trim the stems to 5 cm in length and chop the first 2 cm off the top ends so that the most tender part remains. With your fingers, ease open the leaves so that each artichoke resembles a flower. Heat the oil till very hot (just to smoking point) and fry the artichokes until golden and crisp. Drain on paper towel, sprinkle with salt and pepper and serve hot.

Serves 4.

Carciofi alla Romana

Globe Artichokes Roman Style

4 large artichokes
70 g breadcrumbs
2 cloves garlic
1 small bunch fresh mint
6 tablespoons olive oil
salt and pepper

Time: 1½ hours
Difficulty: +

Trim the artichokes as described in the recipe for Carciofi alla Giudea. Put them in a bowl of cold water containing a little lemon juice (to preserve their green colour).

In a bowl, mix the breadcrumbs with the finely chopped mint and garlic. With your fingers, ease open the artichokes and push the breadcrumb mixture between the leaves. Arrange them side by side in a casserole, sprinkle with salt and pepper and pour the oil on top. Add enough water to come half way up the artichokes and cook slowly until nearly all liquid is evaporated and a fairly thick sauce forms. The artichokes are cooked when the leaves can easily be pulled off.
Serves 4.

Trim artichokes and put them in cold water.

Push breadcrumb mixture between the leaves.

Arrange in a casserole and add water.

Funghi Trifolati

Mushrooms with Garlic and Parsley

800 g field or cultivated mushrooms
100 mL olive oil
3 cloves garlic
salt and pepper
4 tablespoons chopped parsley
juice of half a lemon

Time: 1 hour
Difficulty: +

Wash mushrooms and drain carefully. If they are large, slice them; if small, leave them whole. Warm the oil (it should not be very hot), add garlic cloves and stir once just to warm through. Then add mushrooms and a little salt and pepper and cook for 4–5 minutes on a medium to high heat until they start to form their own liquid. Do not overcook. Take them off the fire, add parsley and lemon juice, lower heat and cook for another 1–2 minutes. Serve hot or cold.
Serves 4.

Carciofi alla Romana

Funghi Trifolati

Spinaci con Uva e Pinoli

Spinach with Pine Nuts and Raisins

1 kg spinach
40 g butter
1 clove garlic
70 g ham
50 g raisins
50 g pine nuts
salt

Time: 1 hour
Difficulty: +

Wash the spinach thoroughly several times, drain and cook in a very little salted water. Drain and squeeze the water out.

Warm butter in a frying pan, add the crushed garlic and the chopped ham, sauté for a few minutes and then add the raisins and pine nuts. Put the spinach in this mixture and stir it around for about 5 minutes, to give time for the flavours to develop. Serve hot.

Serves 4.

Asparagi alla Milanese

Asparagus Milanese Style

In Italy we often serve this asparagus with fried eggs for a light meal.

1.5 kg fresh asparagus
150 g butter
50 g grated Parmesan
salt
freshly ground pepper

Time: 1 hour
Difficulty: +

Clean the asparagus and trim woody ends. Cook in salted boiling water until tender but still retaining a little crispness

(approximately 8–10 minutes). Drain and arrange on a heated serving dish. Heat the butter in a small pan until it becomes light golden brown. Sprinkle the asparagus with the grated Parmesan and pour the butter carefully over. Serve immediately with freshly ground pepper.

Serves 4.

Fagioli all'Uccelletto

Fagioli all'Uccelletto

Beans with Tomato and Sage Sauce

*350 g dried beans
    (borlotti or cannellini)
300 g fresh tomatoes
2 cloves garlic
1 medium-sized bunch
    fresh sage (about 30
    leaves)
120 mL olive oil
salt and freshly ground
    pepper*

*Time: 2½ hours (plus
    time to soak beans)
Difficulty: +*

The tomatoes for this dish can be prepared in one of two ways. Either just chop finely or place whole in boiling water for 1 minute, peel quickly before tomatoes go cold and then purée through sieve or in blender. If using dried beans, soak overnight. The following day, drain them and put them in a pan, cover with cold water and cook for about 2 hours or until soft. Drain.

Warm the oil in a casserole, together with the sage, the crushed garlic and lots of freshly ground pepper. Add the drained beans, salt and sauté on low heat for about 10 minutes. Add the fresh tomato purée and cook for a further 10 minutes. Can be served hot as an accompaniment to grilled meat or roast chicken, or cold as part of a mixed antipasto.

Serves 4.

Note: This dish is also successful with tinned beans.

Crocchette di Patate con Mozzarella

Potato Croquettes with Mozzarella

Mix egg yolks, Parmesan and seasoning into the mashed potato.

Push a cube of ham and one of mozzarella into each croquette.

Coat croquettes with flour, egg and breadcrumbs.

Fry in oil until crisp and golden.

*1 kg potatoes
2 egg yolks
25 g Parmesan
50 g butter
salt and pepper
nutmeg
150 g mozzarella
80 g ham
flour
2 eggs
breadcrumbs
oil*

*Time: 2 hours
Difficulty: ++*

Boil the potatoes in their jackets, peel them and mash them with the butter. Add the two egg yolks, the Parmesan, salt, pepper and nutmeg, and mix well. Shape this mixture into cylinders about 3 cm in diameter and 8 cm in length.

Push into the centre of each one a small cube of mozzarella and one of ham and reshape the croquette so that the mozzarella and ham filling remain in the centre.

Flour the croquettes, dip them in the beaten whole eggs, coat them with breadcrumbs and fry in hot oil till crisp and golden. Serve hot, either with drinks or as an accompaniment to roast meats.

Serves 4.

Finocchi Gratinati

Fennel au Gratin

4 small or *2 large fennel*
  bulbs
100 mL milk
50 g butter
50 g grated Parmesan

Time: 1 hour
Difficulty: +

Discard the outer leaves
and the stalks of the
fennel. Cut the bulbs in
quarters (or eighths,
depending on size). Boil
them in lightly salted
water until *al dente* (still
slightly crisp). Drain them
and arrange in a buttered
ovenproof dish. Sprinkle
the milk on top, cover
with the Parmesan and
dot with the remaining
butter. Put the dish in a
preheated oven at 200°C
(400°F) for 15 minutes or
until nicely golden on top.
Serve hot.
    Serves 4.
    Note: This usually
accompanies more
delicate meats, such as
veal, or egg dishes, as it
has a light, subtle flavour
which can be easily
overpowered.

Zucchine Fritte

Zucchini Chips

800 g zucchini
flour
oil for deep frying
salt

Time: 30 minutes
Difficulty: +

Cut the ends off the
zucchini, wash them and
cut them into chips. Dry
them carefully with paper
towel, roll in flour and
immerse them in very hot
oil until crisp and golden
in colour. Drain on paper
towel, sprinkle with salt
and serve immediately.
    Serves 4.

Cipolline in Agrodolce

Sweet and Sour Shallots

This recipe is also suitable
for baby carrots, baby
squash and small young
turnips. They can be eaten
hot or cold and would
make a lovely addition to
a mixed antipasto.

800 g spring onions
100 g butter
2 teaspoons sugar
2 tablespoons vinegar
salt

Time: 1½ hours
Difficulty: +

Trim the roots and the
green part from the spring
onions, wash them and
drain. Melt the butter in a
casserole, add the spring
onions and sauté until
they start to brown. Add
the sugar, the vinegar and
salt to taste, together with
enough water to just cover
the onions. Continue to
cook slowly until quite
tender, until the liquid is
reduced to a sauce of
coating consistency.
    Serves 4.

Melanzane alla Parmigiana

Kitchenware from The Bay Tree Kitchen Shop

Melanzane alla Parmigiana

Eggplant Parmesan

800 g eggplant
olive oil
100 g Parmesan
2 large mozzarella
400 g freshly made
*   tomato sauce*
4 tablespoons chopped
*   fresh basil*
salt and pepper

Time: 2 hours
Difficulty: ++

Peel the eggplant and cut lengthwise into long thin slices. Salt them and put them in a colander to drain for an hour or more. This is an important step, as it takes the bitterness away from the eggplant. Pat the slices dry and fry them lightly in a little olive oil. Drain on paper towel.

In an oven dish, layer slices of fried eggplant, slices of mozzarella, grated Parmesan, a spoonful or two of tomato sauce, a little basil and so on until you have used all the ingredients. Finish with a little Parmesan and put in the oven at 200°C

(400°F) for 20–30 minutes until a golden crust forms. Serves 4.
Note: This dish can be reheated successfully.

Drain salted eggplant slices in a colander.

Fry eggplant lightly in olive oil.

Arrange ingredients in layers in an ovenproof dish.

Zucca Fritta al Rosmarino

Pumpkin Sauté with Rosemary

800 g pumpkin
100 mL olive oil
few sprigs of rosemary
salt and pepper

Time: 1 hour
Difficulty: +

Peel the pumpkin and cut it in small thick slices. Warm the oil in a frying pan, together with the rosemary. Add the pumpkin slices, a little salt

and pepper and sauté on medium heat until cooked and a little brown. Serve hot.
Serves 4.

Zucchine all'Origano

Zucchini with Oregano

800 g small zucchini
4 tablespoons olive oil
2 cloves garlic
1 teaspoon dry oregano
salt and pepper

Time: 1 hour
Difficulty: +

Cut the ends off the zucchini, wash them and slice them in 2 cm pieces. Warm the oil in a pan with the chopped garlic and add the zucchini. Cook on lively heat, stirring often.

When they are nearly cooked, add salt, pepper and oregano. Continue to sauté until ready. Serve hot.
Serves 4.

MEAT

The Romans used to like their meat seasoned with a mixture of salt and sweet, and honey was used for this purpose. To this day in Italy a little vinegar or wine is added to the cooking juices of meat to sharpen the flavour. Nowhere is this more evident than in the cooking of *abbacchio*, one of the glorious dishes of springtime in the Roman region. The victim for this famous dish is a sucking lamb that has not yet tasted grass, killed at the age of twenty days, and weighing about ten kilograms. It is practically impossible to reproduce this dish in Australia, unless you have a sympathetic butcher who would accept an order to kill a lamb to your requirements.

Another magnificent dish of Italy is Bistecca alla Fiorentina or Beef Steak Florentine Style, which is not really very dissimilar to an Australian or American T-bone steak. It is easy to know which restaurants in Tuscany serve Bistecca as they all display a live charcoal fireplace where the meat will be grilled, amid an explosion of flames and appetising smells.

The slice of meat is enormous (probably 1 kilogram for two persons) and it comes from the vitellone, which is the animal killed when it is no longer a calf, but is not yet beef. It is always served rare, on a warmed plate, garnished with lemon wedges.

Fegato di Vitello alla Veneziana

Calf's Liver and Onion

600 g calf's liver, sliced very thinly
200 g onion, sliced thinly
2 lemons
salt and pepper
4 tablespoons olive oil

Time: 1 hour
Difficulty: +

Fry the onion in the olive oil, stirring continuously until brown. Add the liver and continue cooking on a high heat for a further 2–3 minutes. Do not overcook the liver or it will become tough. Just before serving, add salt and plenty of freshly ground pepper.

Decorate the dish with slices of lemon and accompany this delicious and fast dish with sauté potatoes.
Serves 4.

Arrosto di Vitello alla Parmense

Veal Pot-Roast with Spinach Stuffing

1 loin of veal, boned (about 1.2 kg)
50 g butter
oil
1 glass dry white wine (or water and stock cubes)
salt and pepper

For the stuffing
1 bunch spinach
40 g butter
4 eggs
2 tablespoons grated Parmesan
salt and pepper
80 g bacon

Time: 2½ hours
Difficulty: ++

To prepare the stuffing, wash the spinach and trim the woody ends. Cook it in a very little water, not even enough to cover the spinach, for about 8–10 minutes. Squeeze it dry and mix through it 20 g butter and a little salt.

Beat the eggs in a bowl, add the grated Parmesan and a little salt and pepper. Heat the remaining butter in a pan and make an omelette. Let it get cold.

Open the loin of veal on the table and, with a meat mallet, shape it and flatten it as much as possible. Cover the meat with strips of bacon, and the cold whole omelette. On this arrange a bed of spinach and roll the meat up firmly to form a roll. Sew the raw edges together with a big needle and thick thread. Heat the butter and a couple of tablespoons of oil in a thick casserole and, when hot, brown the meat all over on a lively heat. Add the white wine, let it evaporate, cover the casserole and continue to cook on a very low heat for about 1¼ hours,

basting now and then with the cooking juices. If the roast becomes too dry, add a few tablespoons of broth now and then.

When cooked, correct the seasoning and arrange the meat on a wooden board. Let it rest for 5 minutes before carving in neat slices. Serve hot or cold with a salad.
Serves 4.
Note: This is also delicious with 500 g finely sliced zucchini sautéd in butter instead of spinach.

Ossobuco alla Milanese

Shin of Veal Milanese Style

Italians, like most Europeans, consider bone marrow a great delicacy, and either suck it out or scoop it out with a special spoon.

ossobuco or shin of veal cut into 8 × 5 cm slices
flour
80 g butter
1 very small onion
1 small carrot
1 small piece celery
salt and pepper
1 clove garlic
1 glass white wine
1 × 500 g can peeled tomatoes

250 mL broth (can be made with stock cubes)

For the gremolata
4 tablespoons parsley
1 clove garlic
grated peel of 1 lemon or orange

Time: 2 hours
Difficulty: ++

Flour the ossobuco and brown the slices in the butter. In the meantime slice thinly the onion, carrot, celery and garlic and add to the pan. Season with salt and pepper. Stir occasionally, turning veal to seal it. When everything in the pan has acquired a lovely golden colour, add the wine and let it evaporate almost completely. Now add the sieved tomatoes and cook slowly for just over 1 hour or until you see that the meat is so tender that it falls easily from the bone. If the sauce becomes too thick, add a few tablespoons of broth.

Before serving, lift out the ossobuco and arrange on a heated serving dish. Make a gremolata by chopping finely the parsley with the garlic and adding the lemon or orange peel. Add the gremolata to the sauce in the pan, stir it through and pour over the ossobuco.

Traditionally, ossobuco is served with Risotto alla Milanese (see recipe on p. 23).

Serves 4.

Add thinly sliced vegetables to the browned veal.

When wine has evaporated add the sieved tomatoes.

Finely chop parsley and garlic, and mix with grated peel.

Saltimbocca alla Romana

'Jump into the Mouth'

12 thin veal escalopes
12 slices raw or cooked ham
12 sage leaves or
1 teaspoon dried sage
flour
80 g butter
1 glass white wine or Marsala
salt and pepper

Time: 1 hour
Difficulty: +

Flatten the escalopes with a meat mallet to make them as thin as possible. On each escalope place a slice of ham and sage leaf (or sprinkle with dried sage), fold them in two and secure each envelope with a toothpick. Flour lightly. Heat the butter in a heavy frying pan, and when foaming add the Saltimbocca. Cook on a lively heat for a few minutes until they are brown all over (about 10–12 minutes each side). Now add the white wine or Marsala and let it bubble until it has formed a little sauce. Check the seasoning and serve immediately. Accompany the Saltimbocca with a salad or a green vegetable.

Serves 4.

Olivette di Vitello in Umido con Pisellini

Veal Olives with Peas

12 veal escalopes
12 thin slices ham
100 g mozzarella,
    coarsely grated
12 leaves fresh sage or
    1 teaspoon dried sage
80 g butter
500 g tomatoes, fresh or
    canned
300 g peas, fresh or
    frozen
salt and pepper

Time: 1½ hours
Difficulty: +

Cover each escalope with a slice of ham, sprinkle with grated mozzarella, place a sage leaf on top and roll up to form an olive. Secure with two toothpicks.

When all the olives are ready, sauté them in butter until golden, add the sieved tomatoes, put a lid on the pan and cook slowly for 30 minutes on low to medium heat.

Separately simmer the peas in lightly salted water until cooked. Drain and add to the pan where the veal olives are cooking.

Simmer together for a further 10 minutes and serve hot. This dish is excellent served on a bed of Risotto alla Milanese (see recipe on p. 23).

Serves 4.

Cima alla Genovese

Stuffed Breast of Veal, Genoese Style

This is another lovely cold dish, most suitable for a buffet table. It is fiddly to cook but can be prepared in advance, and you can be certain that it will be a success with your guests.

1 breast of veal (about
    1.2 kg)
200 g calf brains
300 g pork mince, or
    veal and pork mince
100 g fat bacon, minced
2 slices bread, soaked in
    water and squeezed
    out
200 g fresh or frozen
    peas, cooked
40 g grated Parmesan
1 teaspoon dried
    marjoram

1 teaspoon nutmeg
salt and pepper
1 egg
3 hard-boiled eggs,
    shelled
1 carrot
1 onion
1 bay leaf
peppercorns

Time: 3 hours
Difficulty: +++

Ask the butcher to give you a breast of veal without any bones and tell him to cut a large pocket in the breast.

Parboil the brains in salted water, drain and slice thinly. In a large bowl mix together the brains, minced pork, bacon, bread, peas, Parmesan, marjoram, nutmeg, salt and pepper. Bind together with the raw egg. Put some of the mixture in the pocket of the meat. Place the 3 hard-boiled eggs on top inside the pocket and fill the surrounding space with the remaining stuffing mixture. Using a big needle and strong thread, sew together the opening of the pocket. Now take a long piece of string and tie up the meat to give it a regular round shape.

Place the veal in a large pan and cover it with cold water, to which you will add a little salt, the carrot, the onion and the bay leaf and a few peppercorns. Bring it to the boil and simmer for 2 hours. Take it out, put it on a plate and cover with an inverted plate with a weight on top, to compress the veal breast and make the slicing easier. Although this dish is traditionally served cold, it is also delicious hot.

Serves 6–8.

Piccata al Marsala

Veal Escalopes with Marsala

600 g veal escalopes,
    cut very thin
80 g butter
100 mL Marsala
flour
salt and pepper

Time: 30 minutes
Difficulty: +

Flatten the escalopes with a mallet and flour them. Heat the butter in a heavy frying pan, and when foaming, add the veal. Cook them on both sides on high heat until brown. This will only take about 3 minutes. Lift the escalopes out and arrange them on a heated serving dish. To the juices in the pan add the Marsala and let it reduce at high heat until a thickish sauce has formed.

Pour this sauce on the escalopes and serve immediately, accompanied with a potato purée.

Serves 4.

Vitello Tonnato

Veal with Tuna Sauce

1.2 kg veal (a boned
    piece of leg is ideal)
1 carrot
1 onion
2 celery stalks
1 strip lemon or orange
    peel
1½ glasses white wine
150 mL olive oil
salt
200 g can tuna in oil
4 anchovy fillets
375 mL home-made
    mayonnaise
1 tablespoon capers
3 gherkins

Time: 2 hours (plus time
    for chilling)
Difficulty: +++

Roll up the meat and secure with string or toothpicks to maintain its shape and place it in a deep casserole or pan. Add the carrot, the onion, the celery, a strip of lemon peel (or orange peel), the wine, the olive oil and 300 mL cold water. Salt lightly and cook in the oven or on top of the stove for 1 hour or until veal is done. Lift it out and let it get cold.

Strain the cooking liquid and let it reduce until well concentrated. Place the contents of the tin of tuna in a food processor, together with a little of the reduced cooking broth and the anchovy fillets. Let it whirl around for 1 minute and then add the resulting mixture to the home-made mayonnaise. You should obtain a rather runny sauce: if too thick, add a few more spoons of cooking liquid.

Slice the meat and arrange the slices on a serving platter. Pour the sauce on top and decorate with the capers and sliced gherkins. Refrigerate before serving.

Serves 4.

Note: This sauce is also very good on sliced roast veal.

Bollito Misto

Boiled Meat Platter

For very special occasions, and particularly in the north where meat is more abundant and of better quality, the cook might prepare a *bollito misto*. Do not be put off by the idea of boiled meats, as when a variety is cooked and presented together, with various flavours and textures, and colours ranging from cream to pink to brown, it can be a delicious experience.

Serve it with a *salsa verde* or green sauce (see recipe below) or a spicy tomato sauce. The broth can be used for some delicious soup the following day.

1 kg piece of beef
1 pig's trotter
1 cotechino (from
    Italian butchers)
1 capon
1 piece calf's head
1 piece turkey
1 small bunch parsley

2 celery stalks
1 clove garlic
2 onions
3 carrots
2 potatoes
2 zucchini
salt

Time: 3 hours
Difficulty: +

Place the beef, the pig's trotter, the cotechino, the turkey and the capon in boiling water, together with the parsley, celery, garlic, onions and carrots. Add the potatoes and the zucchini and simmer for 1 hour. Now add the calf's head and continue to simmer for a further 2 hours, taking out of the pan the various pieces of meat when you see that they are cooked. Serve all the meats on the same platter, accompanied by a green sauce or tomato sauce.

Serves 8.

Salsa Verde

Green Sauce

1 tablespoon
    breadcrumbs soaked
    in a little vinegar
1 hard-boiled egg, finely
    chopped
2 anchovy fillets
3 tablespoons finely
    chopped parsley
2 tablespoons capers,
    chopped
1 clove garlic

olive oil
lemon juice
salt and pepper

Time: 30 minutes
Difficulty: +

In a small bowl or sauceboat, combine the breadcrumbs, the egg, the anchovy fillets, the parsley, the capers and the crushed garlic clove. Add enough olive oil to achieve the consistency of a rather thin mayonnaise. Add lemon juice to taste and adjust seasoning. This sauce tastes better if prepared a couple of hours in advance.

Serves 6.

Arrosto di Vitello alla Forestiera

Veal Pot-Roast with Stuffing

1 loin of veal, boned
   (about 1.2 kg)
1 small onion
100 g bacon
oil
1 glass dry white wine
250 mL broth (can be
   made with stock
   cubes)
30 g butter
salt and pepper

For the stuffing
200 g minced beef
150 g sausage mince
1 bread roll
200 mL milk
1 tablespoon pistachio
   nuts
2 tablespoons chopped
   parsley
1 egg

salt and pepper
60 g Parmesan

Time: 3 hours
Difficulty: ++

To prepare the stuffing, first soak the bread in milk. Put the pistachios in boiling water for 1 minute, drain and peel. In a bowl, mix together the minced beef, the sausage mince, the soaked and squeezed-out bread, the parsley and the pistachio nuts, the egg, grated Parmesan, salt and pepper.

Open the loin of veal on the table and flatten with a meal mallet to shape it. Spread the stuffing on top, roll up the meat firmly to form a big roll and sew the untidy ends together with a big needle and thick thread. Place the meat in a heavy casserole with the sliced onion, chopped bacon, butter and oil. Let the meat brown all over on a lively heat. Add the white wine, let it evaporate, cover the casserole and continue to cook on very low heat for about 1¼ hours, basting now and then with the cooking juices. If the roast becomes too dry, add a few tablespoons of broth now and then.

Check for salt and pepper and place the meat on a wooden board. Let it rest for five minutes before carving in neat slices. Serve it with its own cooking juices, accompanied with roast potatoes or peas cooked in butter.

Serves 4.

Braciole di Vitello al Rosmarino

Veal Chops with Rosemary

4 large or 8 small veal
   chops
50 g butter
1 sprig rosemary
½ glass Madeira or
   sherry
1 stock cube
salt and pepper

Time: 1 hour
Difficulty: +

Chop the rosemary and place it in a heavy pan with the butter. When the butter is just colouring, place the chops in the pan and sauté until well browned. Sprinkle the Madeira or sherry on top and the stock cube dissolved in a little water.

Shake the pan from time to time, until the meat is tender. Serve with its own juices and accompany it with a dish of lightly cooked spinach.

Serves 4.

Arista di Maiale alla Toscana

Roast Pork with Fennel

Arista is the Tuscan name for a loin of pork.

1 pork loin
2 teaspoons fennel seeds
8 sage leaves
2 cloves garlic
salt and pepper
oil

Time: 2 hours
Difficulty: +

With a small knife, make a number of slits in the meat at regular intervals, and in each one insert some fennel seeds, a little piece of sage and a slice of garlic. Salt and pepper the pork and moisten the skin with olive oil. Roast in a preheated oven at 225°C (425°F) until the juices run clear. Serve hot, cut in slices. In Tuscany, the traditional accompaniment to arista is freshly cooked dried beans, served hot, seasoned with oil, salt and pepper.

Serves 4.

Costolette di Maiale alla Pizzaiola

Pork Chops with Pizzaiola Sauce

4 pork chops
40 g butter
oil
2 cloves garlic
1 teaspoon oregano
250 g tomatoes, peeled
  and chopped, or half
  a can peeled
  tomatoes
salt and pepper

Time: 1 hour
Difficulty: ++

Season the pork chops with salt and pepper and sauté them in butter to which you have added a little oil. When they are golden all over and cooked through, arrange them on a serving plate and keep warm. To the juices in the pan, add the crushed garlic, oregano and tomato. Correct the seasoning if necessary, and let it warm through. Put this sauce on the chops and serve immediately.

Serves 4.

Maiale in Salsa di Noci

Pork with Walnut Sauce

1.2 kg loin of pork
salt and pepper
250 mL broth (can be
  made with stock
  cubes)
4 shallots
6 tablespoons fresh
  cream
100 g walnuts, very
  finely chopped
1 teaspoon butter
1 teaspoon flour

1 tablespoon Cognac or
  other brandy
1 tablespoon chopped
  parsley

Time: 2 hours
Difficulty: +

Salt and pepper the loin and roast in the oven at 190°C (375°F) until cooked to your taste. Pour off the fat, leaving the juices in the pan, add a cupful of broth (or water and stock cube) and let it reduce while continually scraping the bottom of the pan. Add the fresh cream and the walnuts and continue stirring for 2 minutes. Amalgamate the butter with the flour and add it to the gravy in the pan, together with the brandy. Simmer while stirring until the sauce thickens.

Slice the meat on a serving plate and pour a little of the sauce on top. Sprinkle with the chopped parsley and chopped shallots. Serve hot, with the remaining sauce separate.

Serves 4.

Maiale al Latte

Pork Baked in Milk

This is a particularly good way to bake a nice piece of pork or veal, as the milk will keep the meat moist and at the same time form a delicious sauce. If you prefer to cook this dish in the oven, reduce the quantity of milk by half.

1.2 kg boned pork from
  the leg or loin
60 g butter
100 g onion

Tie the meat to form a large sausage. In a deep pan, sauté the onion, carrot and celery, all finely chopped, in the

1 small carrot
1 celery stalk
2 sprigs parsley
400 mL milk
salt and pepper

Time: 2 hours
Difficulty: ++

butter. When they are translucent, place on top of this mixture the parsley sprigs and on top of this the meat. Brown it to seal all the juices, season, pour the milk over and put a lid on the pan. Cook slowly for about 2 hours, without stirring. At the end of the cooking, you will see that the milk has formed a lovely golden sauce around the meat. The only point at which this dish needs watching is towards the end of the cooking, because if the milk evaporates too much, it may stick to the pan and burn. It can be eaten, with the sauce poured over it, hot or cold.

Serves 4.

Abbacchio all'Aceto

Baby Lamb with Vinegar and Anchovy Sauce

Abbacchio is a very young and tender milk-fed lamb. The nearest Australian equivalent is young spring lamb.

1.2 kg boneless spring
  lamb from leg or
  shoulder, cut in large
  cubes
4 anchovy fillets
2 cloves garlic
1 small glass wine
  vinegar or 3
  tablespoons cider
  vinegar and 1 small
  glass wine
4 tablespoons olive oil
flour
1 large sprig fresh
  rosemary
salt and freshly ground
  pepper

Time: 1½ hours
Difficulty: +

In a small bowl, crush the garlic with the anchovy fillets and dilute the mixture with the vinegar, or vinegar and wine.

In a heavy pan, warm the oil, and when it is just beginning to smoke, add the lightly floured lamb pieces and the rosemary. Sauté until well browned, then lower the heat and cover the pan and continue to cook until tender. If during the cooking the meat becomes too dry, add a few tablespoons of water. Ten minutes before the end of cooking, add to the pan the anchovy and vinegar mixture, and mix it through to let the flavours subtly penetrate the meat. Taste for seasoning and serve hot, with the juices.

Traditionally, this dish should be served with a hot potato salad flavoured with anchovies and garlic or with a dish of hot spinach sautéd in butter.

Serves 4–6.

Agnello Imbottito alla Folignate

Stuffed Leg of Lamb

1 medium-sized leg of
  lamb
100 g Italian salami
100 g Italian provolone,
  or tasty Cheddar
1 celery stalk
30 g grated Parmesan
4 tablespoons chopped
  parsley
nutmeg
salt and freshly ground
  pepper
30 g breadcrumbs
2 cloves garlic
2 eggs
oil

Time: 2 hours
Difficulty: ++

In a bowl mix together the salami and provolone, both chopped finely, the grated Parmesan, parsley, celery, nutmeg, salt and pepper, breadcrumbs and crushed garlic. Bind together with the eggs and let it rest for 10 minutes or so. Open the leg of lamb and spread with the stuffing. With a big needle and strong thread, sew the edges together, trying to keep the shape of the leg. Baste the meat with a little oil and bake in a preheated oven at 200°C (400°F) for 1 hour (if you like your lamb pink) or more if well done. Serve cut in slices, with roast potatoes.

Serves 4.

Abbacchio al Forno

Roast Baby Lamb

1 leg baby lamb
1 large sprig rosemary
2 cloves garlic
oil
4 tablespoons wine
  vinegar
flour
3 anchovy fillets
salt and pepper

Time: 1½ hours
Difficulty: ++

Make a number of incisions in the leg of lamb and insert in each a few needles of rosemary and a slice of garlic. Preheat the oven to 190°C (375°F) and bake the meat for 1 hour, or less if you like your lamb pink. Deglaze the pan with the vinegar, make a gravy in the usual way and add to it the chopped anchovies with a clove of garlic. The anchovies and vinegar make an ideal gravy for the lamb.

Serves 4–6.

Costolette di Vitello alla Milanese

Crumbed Veal Chops

4 large or 8 small veal
chops
flour
salt and pepper
2 eggs
breadcrumbs
100 g butter
2 lemons

Time: 1 hour
Difficulty: +

Flatten the cutlets with a meat mallet, season with salt and pepper, flour them, dip them in beaten egg and breadcrumbs and fry them in the butter until golden and cooked through. Do not overcook as they become dry. Arrange them on a plate, pour a little of the cooking butter on top and decorate with lemon wedges. Serve with potato chips (thin slices of whole peeled potatoes fried in very hot oil for 3–5 minutes and drained on paper towel).
Serves 4.

Abbacchio Brodettato

Spring Lamb with Egg Sauce

1.2 kg boneless spring
lamb from the leg or
shoulder, cut in large
cubes
25 g butter
50 g ham
4 shallots
nutmeg
salt and pepper
1 glass white wine
1 tablespoon flour
1 clove garlic
2 tablespoons chopped
parsley
2 egg yolks
juice of half a lemon
2 tablespoons grated
Parmesan

Time: 1½ hours
Difficulty: ++

Heat the butter in a heavy pan, add the finely chopped ham and shallots, a little nutmeg, salt and pepper and sauté for a few minutes. When it starts to colour, add the lamb and let it brown all over. Add the wine and let it evaporate, then the flour, stirring carefully to mix it in and form a little thickened gravy. Now add enough water to make a rather liquid sauce, lower the heat, cover the pan and continue to cook until done. Half way through the cooking add the finely chopped garlic and parsley.

In a small bowl, beat the egg yolks with the lemon juice and the cheese. When the lamb is cooked, take off the stove and add the egg and lemon mixture. Mix it thoroughly and heat through again to thicken it, being careful that the eggs do not scramble. Serve immediately, with a potato purée.
Serves 4.

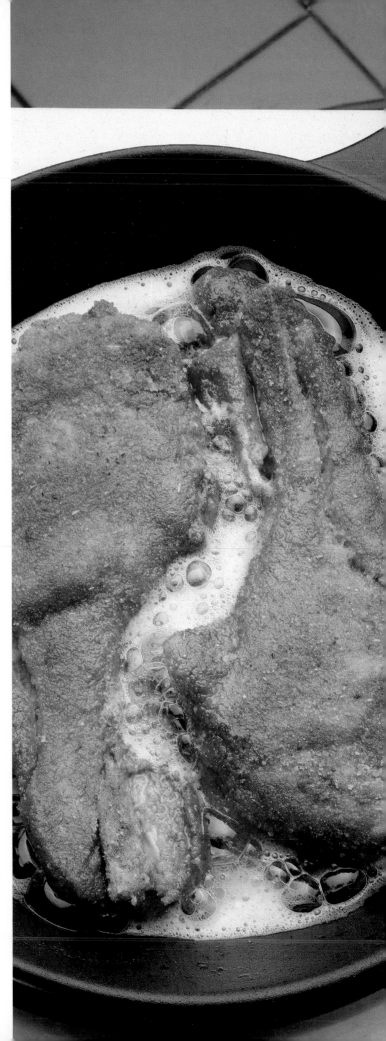

Costolette di Vitello alla Milanese

POULTRY

Italians love to eat anything that flies; from time immemorial, they have enjoyed eating small birds. In Italy, during the hunting season, specialised butchers sell to the public all kinds of birds, plucked and ready to cook. They range from thrushes to robins, ortolans and figpeckers and they are often sold skewered, eight to a skewer, with their little heads in neat rows and feet all pointing in the same direction! I do not think that most Australians would fancy eating the poor little creatures, but in the last few years quails have started to appear in poultry shops, and by now they are commonly available. I have provided one recipe for quail which is very easy and which you might wish to try. I am sure you will have fun trying the chicken and turkey dishes given, as they are all somewhat unusual and most suitable for entertaining.

Arrosto di Quaglie su Crostini

Roast Quails on Croûtons

8 quails
salt and freshly ground pepper
8 shallots
2 celery stalks
8 small sprigs parsley
8 thin slices bacon
300 mL chicken stock (can be made with stock cubes)
100 g butter
8 croûtons, cut from a French stick

Time: 1½ hours
Difficulty: ++

Rub the quails with a little salt and freshly ground pepper. In each one insert a shallot, a small piece celery and a sprig of parsley, and wrap it in a slice of bacon. Tie each one with a piece of string to keep its shape during cooking. Butter an oven dish large enough to accommodate the quails. Put in the oven at 200°C (400°F) for 25 minutes. When cooked, take off the string and arrange on a serving dish. Keep warm.

Deglaze the cooking pan with the chicken stock and let it reduce to half its quantity. Off the heat, add the butter, mixing thoroughly to form a creamy sauce. Add more freshly ground pepper. Fry the croûtons in a little butter and put a quail on each croûton. Serve hot, with the butter sauce poured over the top.

Serves 4.

Pollo coi Peperoni

Chicken with Capsicums

1 × 1.6 kg chicken
4 green capsicums
800 g fresh peeled tomatoes
1 large onion
30 g butter
2 tablespoons oil
1 glass white wine
salt and pepper
3 tablespoons fresh chopped basil leaves

Time: 2 hours
Difficulty: +

Grill the capsicums or, if you have a gas stove, hold them over the flame with a fork until the skin blackens and blisters. Rub off the skin, wash the capsicums, seed them and cut in strips.

Cut the tomatoes in chunks and slice the onion. Cut the chicken in smallish pieces.

Heat the butter and oil in a heavy frying pan or large casserole and add the onion and the chicken. Sauté until brown. Now add the wine, let it evaporate for a minute, and add the capsicums and the tomatoes. Put a lid on the pan and let it simmer until cooked, about 30 minutes, adding some water if necessary. Serve hot sprinkled with fresh chopped basil.

Serves 4.

Filetti di Pollo Rossini

Chicken Breasts Rossini

4 breasts of chicken
4 slices of foie gras or, if available, 4 slices of fresh goose liver (a very good pâté is a fair substitute)
70 g butter
flour
1 small glass port or Madeira
salt and pepper

Time: 1 hour
Difficulty: +

Spread the chicken breasts on the table. On each one put a slice of foie gras. If using fresh goose liver, seal the slices for a minute in butter on high heat before you put them on the chicken breasts. Fold each breast in two, so that you have a kind of chicken roll. Flour the rolls and sauté in butter on a lively heat. As soon as they are cooked (this will take no more than 10 minutes), arrange them on a heated serving dish. Add the Madeira or port to the juices in the pan to form a rich brown sauce. Pour the sauce on the chicken rolls and serve immediately.
Serves 4.

Pollo al Cacciatore

Chicken Cacciatore

2 kg chicken pieces
flour seasoned with salt and pepper
125 mL oil
1 clove garlic
2 onions
2 green peppers
4 cups canned whole tomatoes
125 mL tomato purée
3 tablespoons tomato paste
2 teaspoons salt
1 teaspoon sugar
freshly cracked pepper
1 sprig fresh thyme (or 1 teaspoon dried)
½ teaspoon mixed spice
½ cup red cooking wine
12 black olives
finely chopped parsley

Time: 1½ hours
Difficulty: ++

Coat chicken pieces with seasoned flour and brown in hot oil. Stir in the crushed garlic, diced onions and chopped green pepper and cook for 10 minutes on low heat. Add tomatoes, tomato purée and tomato paste, salt, sugar, cracked black pepper, thyme and mixed spice. Stir until combined and cook uncovered for 15–20 minutes on a low flame.

Add the wine, cover and cook for 45 minutes or until chicken is tender and a thick sauce has formed.

Before serving toss in the black olives and sprinkle with finely chopped parsley.
Serves 6–8.

Pollo Fritto alla Fiorentina

Fried Chicken Florentine Style

1 × 1.6 kg chicken
oil
2 lemons
a little chopped parsley
1 clove garlic
1 sprig rosemary
1 bay leaf
salt and pepper

For the batter
2 eggs
2 tablespoons flour
milk
salt
pinch cayenne pepper

Time: 2 hours
Difficulty: +

Make a marinade with 4 or 5 tablespoons olive oil, the juice of 1 lemon, parsley, the chopped rosemary and bay leaf, the crushed garlic, salt and pepper. Cut the chicken in smallish pieces and marinate for about 1 hour, turning occasionally.

Now make a batter by mixing the eggs, the flour and enough milk to give a mixture with the texture of thickened cream. Season with salt and cayenne pepper and let it rest for 10 minutes.

Drain the chicken pieces from the marinade and dip them in the batter. Fry them in hot oil until golden. Drain on paper towel and salt lightly. Arrange on a serving plate and serve with lemon wedges. A home-made tomato sauce can be passed around separately.
Serves 4.

Fricassea di Pollo all'Antica

Old-fashioned Chicken Casserole

1 × 1.6 kg chicken
100 g butter
20 g flour
600 mL broth (can be
  made with stock
  cubes)
salt and pepper
nutmeg
1 sprig thyme
1 bay leaf
few sprigs parsley
200 g spring onions
200 g button
  mushrooms
2 egg yolks
100 mL fresh cream

Time 2 hours
Difficulty: ++

Joint the chicken into 8 or more pieces. Warm 40 g butter in a casserole and put in the chicken pieces. Sprinkle with the flour, and stir through for a few seconds. Now add the broth, salt, pepper and nutmeg and the herbs. Cover the casserole and simmer gently for 30 minutes.

In the meantime, in a smaller pan, warm 30 g butter and simmer in it the onions and mushrooms until cooked, adding a few tablespoons of water as necessary.

In a small bowl, beat the egg yolks, add the fresh cream and 2 tablespoons of the liquid from the mushrooms. Put the egg mixture in the chicken casserole and stir through carefully on extremely low heat, so that the eggs will not scramble. Take it off the stove and let it rest for a minute or two before serving.

Serves 4.

Pollo alla Diavola

Barbecued Chicken

This is a dish to be found often in restaurants in Tuscany and elsewhere, where it is always grilled on a charcoal or wood fire. At home it can be done on the grill of a stove.

2 young chickens
  (1–1.2 kg each)
oil or butter
salt and pepper

Time: 30 minutes
Difficulty: +

Cut each chicken in two and brush each half with oil or melted butter. Grill it on a barbecue or domestic grill, being careful that it does not dry out. Salt and pepper at the end of the cooking. Serve it simply as it is, with a green salad.

Serves 4.

Filetti di Tacchino alla Bolognese

Turkey Fillets Bolognese Style

4 turkey fillets
flour
salt and pepper
2 eggs
breadcrumbs
50 g butter
4 slices Gruyère, the
  same size as the fillets

4 slices prosciutto or
  ham

Time: 1 hour
Difficulty: +

Flour the fillets, salt them lightly and dip them in beaten egg and then in breadcrumbs. Fry them in the butter until golden. Now put on each fillet a slice of ham and top with a slice of cheese. Transfer to an ovenproof dish and put in a preheated oven at 200°C (400°F) until the cheese has melted. Serve hot.

Serves 4.

Note: This recipe is also suitable for chicken breasts.

Filetti di Tacchino Fritti al Limone

Fried Turkey Breasts with Lemon

4 turkey fillets
flour
2 eggs
breadcrumbs
70 g butter
2 lemons

handful of chopped
  parsley

Time: 1 hour
Difficulty: +

Flour the fillets and dip them in the beaten eggs and then in breadcrumbs. Fry in butter until golden. Serve hot with wedges of lemon and chopped parsley.

Serves 4.

Note: This recipe is also suitable for chicken breasts.

SWEETS AND ICE CREAMS

Italians have been known for centuries for their deftness at preparing sweets and pastry, and traditionally the courts of Europe would employ Italian confectioners for their tables. It was the Venetian traders who first imported and commercialised sugar in Europe, where it remained for a long time a treat for the very rich; the common people had to make do with honey.

Most cities have their particular sweet: there is *panforte* in Siena, *panettone* in Milan, *pastiera* in Naples, *amaretti* in Perugia, *cassata* in Sicily and so on. Also all the more popular saints have a sweetmeat which is avidly consumed on their name-day, such as *zeppole* for St Joseph, who is the patron of Italy. Then there is *frittole* for Easter, *pinoccate* for the Epiphany, *fave* for All Saints, and so on.

Most of these sweets are extremely tricky to make and most Italians prefer to leave it to the professional pastrycook. At home at the end of a meal, often the dessert consists of a basket of fresh fruit and perhaps some of the above or other sweets bought from the corner patisserie. For special occasions, the hostess might prepare an ice cream or zabaglione or a dessert based on fruit, and this has been my guideline in the selection of the following recipes, which are all fairly simple to make and appealing to the eye as well as the palate.

Cassata alla Siciliana

Sicilian Cassata

This is a homely and delicious version of this most famous Sicilian sweet.

700 g very fresh ricotta
200 g sugar
150 g candied lemon
    peel
100 g cooking chocolate
4 (or more) tablespoons
    rum
400 g sponge cake or
    sponge fingers

Time: 1 hour (plus refrigeration time)
Difficulty: ++

Using a large bowl and a wooden spoon, cream the ricotta until very smooth, add the sugar, 1 tablespoon rum, the candied peel and the chocolate chopped in very small pieces. Sprinkle the remaining rum on the sponge cake (or sponge fingers) and line the bottom and sides of a mould or soufflé dish. Fill the mould with the ricotta mixture and refrigerate for at least three hours before serving. If you wish to unmould the cassata, line the mould with greaseproof paper brushed with rum.
    Serves 6.

Add candied peel and chocolate to the creamed ricotta.

Line mould with sponge cake or fingers.

Fill mould with the ricotta mixture.

Pinoccate

Pine Nut Macaroons

500 g sugar
300 g ground almonds
4 egg whites
1 teaspoon vanilla
   essence
200 g pine nuts

Time: 2 hours
Difficulty: ++

In a food processor place the sugar, ground almonds, vanilla and egg whites. Whirl for a minute or so, to form a smooth paste. Mix the whole pine nuts into this mixture and with the help of a spoon form little mounds the size of a walnut on an oiled biscuit tray. Dry in the oven at 160°C (325°F) for 10–12 minutes.
   Serves 4–6.

Blend sugar, ground almonds, vanilla and egg whites.

Place walnut-sized spoonfuls on a greased biscuit tray.

Stir in pine nuts.

Tartufi al Cioccolato

Chocolate Truffles

250 g bitter chocolate
100 g butter
3 egg yolks
2 tablespoons milk
60 g cocoa

Time: 1 hour
Difficulty: +

Melt the chocolate in a double boiler with the milk. When it is hot, take it off the fire and work in the butter and the egg yolks. Let this mixture get cold. Form it into small walnut shapes and coat with the cocoa. These truffles should be eaten within two or three days.

Melone Marinato

Marinated Rock Melon

1 rock melon
4 tablespoons Marsala
   or port
1 tablespoon sugar
1 punnet raspberries
   (optional)

Time: 1 hour
Difficulty: +

With a melon baller, scoop out melon flesh and transfer to a glass bowl. Add raspberries if used, sprinkle with sugar and Marsala or port and refrigerate before serving.
   Serves 4.

Crostata di Ciliege

Cherry Shortcake

For the pastry
300 g flour
150 g butter
150 g sugar
grated peel of 1 lemon
2 eggs
pinch of salt

For the filling
800 g dark red cherries,
stoned
1 small jar cherry jam
2 tablespoons icing
sugar

Time: 2½ hours
Difficulty: ++

To prepare the pastry, sift flour onto a board, add salt, sugar and the grated lemon peel, mix together and make a well in the centre. Break in 1 egg and add the butter cut in pieces. Knead with the fingertips, taking care not to work the pastry too much. When smooth, shape into a ball, roll in buttered greaseproof paper and refrigerate for 30 minutes. Roll the pastry out to a thickness of 5 mm and line a tart or quiche dish which you have previously buttered and floured. Using a pastry wheel, cut the leftover pastry into long ribbons.

Spread the cherry jam on the bottom of the pastry and cover with the washed and stoned cherries. Sprinkle with the icing sugar and ribbons.

Brush the pastry with beaten egg. Bake in a pre-heated oven at 180°C (350°F) for 45 minutes. Serve hot or cold.
    Serves 6.

Shape pastry dough into a ball.

Line a tart or quiche dish.

Spread pastry with cherry jam and cover with stoned cherries.

Crostata di Fichi

Fresh Fig Shortcake

1 quantity short pastry
(see Cherry Shortcake
recipe)
500 g fresh figs
1 small jar raspberry
jam
50 g sugar
2 tablespoons
maraschino

Line a baking dish with the pastry. Peel the figs and macerate them for about 30 minutes in the maraschino and sugar. Proceed as for Cherry Shortcake.

Crostata della Nonna

Grandmother's Shortcake

*1 quantity short pastry
(see Cherry Shortcake
recipe)
300 g ricotta
100 g amaretti or
macaroon biscuits
70 g sugar
50 g raisins
50 g bitter chocolate,
grated
2 egg yolks
2 tablespoons Amaretto
liqueur or rum*

Line a baking dish with
the pastry. In a bowl,
cream the ricotta with the
sugar, add the crushed
biscuits, liqueur, raisins,
chocolate and egg yolks.
Fill the lined baking dish
with this mixture,
decorate with pastry
ribbons and bake for 45
minutes. Serve cold.

Crostoli, Chiacchiere, Frappe, Cenci

Sweet Fritters

These are basically the
same sweet with different
regional names. They are
our typical Lent sweet,
when all flour, sugar and
oil should be used up
before forty days of
fasting. The English and
Irish pancakes have of
course the same origin.

*350 g flour
50 g butter
20 g sugar
2 eggs
1 teaspoon vanilla
essence
pinch salt
oil for deep frying
(peanut or sunflower)
icing sugar*

*Time: 2 hours
Difficulty: +*

Combine the flour, butter,
sugar, eggs, vanilla and
pinch of salt and knead
into a smooth soft dough.
Shape it into a ball, cover
it with a kitchen towel and
let it rest for an hour or so.

With a rolling pin, roll
the dough out very thinly
(the thickness of a 20 cent
piece). Cut into ribbons
and twist in bows,
butterflies, or whatever
shape takes your fancy.
Heat enough oil for deep
frying and drop the
crostoli in a few at a time
until golden and a little
puffed. Drain on paper
towel, sprinkle with icing
sugar and serve hot or
cold. They are an ideal
accompaniment for
Pesche allo Spumante (see
p. 93). Zabaglione (see
p. 95) or ice creams.
Serves 4.

Roll the dough out very thinly.

Cut rolled dough into ribbons or twist
into bows.

Deep fry crostoli until puffed and
golden.

Arance al Caramello

Caramelised Oranges

200 g sugar
40 g butter
4 large oranges (navels)
*4 tablespoons toasted
   slivered almonds*

Time: 2 hours
Difficulty: ++

Dissolve sugar over low
heat, stirring constantly,
and simmer until syrup is
a golden colour. Remove
from heat; add butter and
stir until smooth. Peel the
oranges, removing all pith
and white membrane.
Slice thinly and arrange
on a serving dish in
overlapping layers. Pour
the sauce over them and
sprinkle with almonds.
Serve with whipped
cream, if wished.
   Serves 4.

Gelato alle Nocciole

Hazelnut Ice Cream

4 egg yolks
200 g sugar
100 g ground hazelnuts
500 mL milk

Time: 1½ hours
Difficulty: +++

Bring the milk to the boil,
stir in the hazelnuts and
let it infuse until the milk
gets cold. Strain through
muslin or a very fine
sieve.
   Beat the egg yolks with
the sugar until creamy and
forming a ribbon. Add the
milk and put in the top of
a double boiler on low
heat. Continue to beat
until it reaches boiling
point. Let it get cold.
Freeze as in Gelato alla
Crema Zabaglione.
   Serves 4.

Pesche allo Spumante

Peaches in Spumante

*4 perfectly matured
   freestone peaches*
a little icing sugar
*1 bottle good quality dry
   Italian spumante (or
   French champagne)*

Time: 1 hour
Difficulty: +

Drop the peaches in
boiling water for 30
seconds, take them out
and peel them. The
contact with boiling water
makes the peeling process
easier, as the skin will
detach from the flesh.
   Cut each peach in half
and take out the stone.
Sprinkle each half with a
little icing sugar and let it
rest for no more than 5
minutes, or peach will go
black. Take four large
champagne glasses and
arrange in each one 2
peach halves. Fill up the
glass with Italian
spumante or champagne
and serve. Serve with
crostoli (p. 90).
   Serves 4.

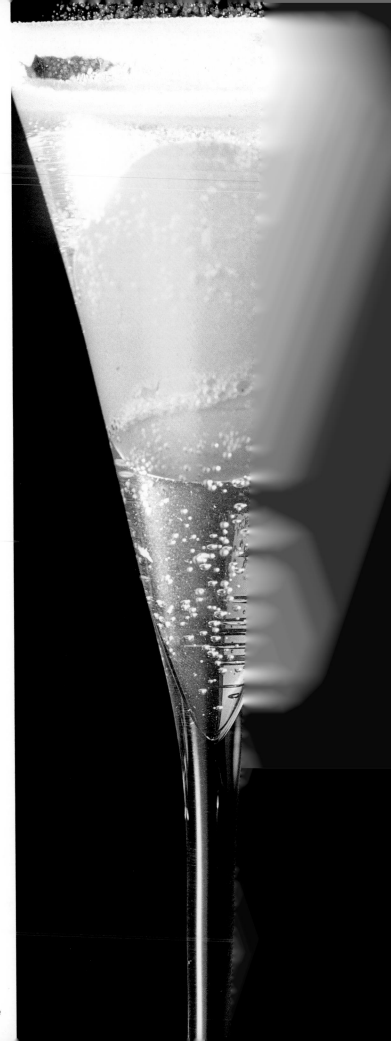

Arance al Caramello   Pesche allo Spumante

Fragole al Vino Rosso

Strawberries in Red Wine

400 g fresh strawberries
150 g sugar
1 lemon
1 glass red wine

Time: 30 minutes (plus refrigeration time)
Difficulty: +

Hull and wash strawberries, drain carefully and arrange in a glass bowl. Refrigerate for 2 hours. Mix the wine and lemon juice, and add sugar. Stir to dissolve sugar. A little while before serving, pour the wine mixture on the strawberries.
   Serves 4.

Gelato all'Anguria

Watermelon Ice Cream

250 g watermelon flesh, with seeds removed
250 g sugar
100 mL fresh cream

Time: 1 hour (plus refrigeration time)
Difficulty: ++

Melt the sugar in 500 mL of warm water and let it boil for 2 minutes. Mash the watermelon flesh and add to it the whipped cream. Fold the watermelon and whipped cream mixture into the syrup. Freeze as in the recipe for Gelato alla Crema Zabaglione.
   Serves 4.

Zabaglione

4 egg yolks
100 g sugar
8 tablespoons dry Marsala
grated peel of half a lemon

Time: 30 minutes
Difficulty: ++

Put the egg yolks and sugar in a bowl and beat until the mixture forms a ribbon. Add the lemon peel and Marsala and place the bowl over heat in a double boiler. Keep beating with a whisk or egg beater until you have obtained a rich, frothy consistency, and the volume of the eggs has doubled. Pour into wine glasses and serve hot.

Accompany with home-made biscuits, such as pinoccate.
   Serves 4.

Gelato alla Crema Zabaglione

Zabaglione Ice Cream

4 egg yolks
200 g sugar
500 mL milk
100 mL Marsala

Time: 1 hour (plus refrigeration time)
Difficulty: +++

In a bowl, beat the yolks with the sugar until creamy and forming a ribbon. Place the bowl in a double boiler, add the milk and continue beating until very hot. Let the mixture cool.

If you have an ice cream maker, pour the mixture into it and churn until frozen. Otherwise, pour the mixture into ice cube trays and place in the freezer. Stir it through after the first hour, to break up any icy particles that might have formed, and finish the freezing process. Serve with crostoli.
   Serves 4.

Index

Printed in Singapore